HIS POWER

Living in Step with the Holy Spirit

HIS POWER

Living in Step with the Holy Spirit

Mike Ellicott
with C. S. Ellicott

Sweetwater Still Publishing
Colcord, Oklahoma USA

Visit Sweetwater Still Publishing at
www.sweetwaterstill.com

ISBN: 978-0-9843599-6-7
LCCN: 2018906267
Published by Sweetwater Still Publishing
Colcord, Oklahoma USA

Printed in the United States of America
22 21 20 19 18 / 11 10 9 8 7 6 5 4 3 2

Contents

FOREWORD

In this day of superficial Christianity, cheap grace, self-improvement, and perverted theology, it's refreshing to read a book based on the pure, unadulterated Word of God.

As I read through *'His Power'* this little poem of John Bunyan's came to mind.

> *Run John run the Law demands,*
> *But gives us neither feet nor hands.*
> *Far better news the gospel brings,*
> *It bids us fly and gives us wings.*

The author, Mike Ellicott, shares how for years he struggled with living the life of a Christian in his own strength; only to find it impossible. Trying to keep the Law without 'feet or hands' was never God's plan. Joseph Alleine wrote in 1671 the following:

> "Never think you can convert yourself. If ever you would be savingly converted, you must despair of doing it in your own strength. It is a resurrection from the dead (Eph 2:1), a new creation (Gal 6:15, Eph 2:10), a work of absolute omnipotence. (Eph 1:19) Are not these out

of reach of human power? If you have no more than you had by your first birth, a good nature, a meek and chaste temper etc., you are a stranger to true conversion. This is a supernatural work."

The good news of the gospel, as Bunyan describes it, is that God provides us the 'wings to fly'. This power to fly is only available through the empowering work of the Holy Spirit. Mike shares with us how he discovered this life changing principle of dying to self and letting God have His way daily in his life.

If, like Mike, you're sick and tired of trying and failing, trying and failing, then this book is for you. Follow Mike on his personal journey to true freedom and discover what the Prophet Isaiah found when he wrote:

"But those who trust in the Lord will find new strength.
They will soar high on wings like eagles.
They will run and not grow weary.
They will walk and not faint."
Isaiah 40:31 NLT

David Ravenhill,
Teacher, Author

INTRODUCTION

A lot of people use the phrase *What Would Jesus Do?*
Some of them even have the *WWJD* bracelets to remind
themselves to ask this question before making a decision. I've heard this concept taught from many pulpits.
The preacher explains a passage of scripture and then
leaves me with, "This is how you need to live."

Here's what Jesus would do; you should do it too.

I agree! I really *should* do what Jesus would do! But the
Scripture just described behavior that's the opposite of
my own nature. God is right and I'm wrong. But how
can I act like Jesus, when I'm not Jesus? Even when I try
my hardest to act like Him, I can't do it.

This dilemma leads many to unbelief, and it's caused
by lack of understanding. We're taught that Jesus died
to save us. But what does that mean exactly? Anytime
we're saved *from* something, we're saved *to* something
else. For example: I'm drowning under the water and a
lifeguard comes to save me—he saves me *from* under-
water *to* the dry land.

In the matter of the salvation of our souls, we're told
that we can be saved. But we're not always told what

we're being saved *from* and what we're being saved *to*. What am I floating in, anyway?

Contrary to popular belief, the pool isn't my sin. It's my nature. And I was born *face down* in it. I've been floating here for a long, long time. Powerless and drifting with the currents, I've only become more rotten with time. Now along comes a preacher who tells me to act like Jesus.

Can you see the absurdity? This is the problem with being taught what the Bible says I should do, but not being told how to perform these miracles.

This is the dilemma Paul spoke of in Romans Chapter Seven. Thankfully, Paul didn't leave us in that chapter, but moved on in Chapter Eight to explain the new life of the believer—a resurrected life, raised and empowered by the Holy Spirit of God.

We're living in a time when the church is most often being taught only half of the gospel. But half of the good news isn't good news at all. We need the entire gospel message! In addition to what you're about to read in this book, here are some authors and books I highly recommend: Andrew Murray, *Absolute Surrender*; Roy Hession, *The Calvary Road*; David Ravenhill, *Blood Bought*; Roy Lessin, *The Holy Spirit Book*.

Mike Ellicott, 2018

"To be controlled by human
nature results in death.

To be controlled by the Spirit
results in life and peace."

Romans 8:9

The Natural

What if you find out what God wants from you, but you don't want to do it? Or maybe you want to please Him, but it seems impossible?

Do you believe Jesus died on a cross as punishment for your sin? Do you believe He rose after three days—proving that He's God and that He can forgive sin? Have you asked Him to forgive you and made Him Lord over your life? If you answered yes, you're a *believer*. After believing, the Bible commands us to find out what the Lord wants us to do. But then what?

What if you find out what the Lord wants—but you can't do it?

God's grace gives me the power to perform the things that are otherwise impossible for me. God's grace even gives me a desire to do things that go against my natural wishes. Throughout this book, we'll study what the Bible says about this. I pray you will not spend wasted years (like I did) calling yourself a Christian while feeling like you should tag on a disclaimer:

"I'm a believer. But I'm not living up to it."

I'll also tell you some stories from my life. Maybe if you see how hard-headed I've been, you won't need to duplicate it. You can learn from my mistakes.

So what if you find out what the Lord wants, and you're stuck there? Regardless of who we are or what we know, we all start our faith journey with ideas about what we ought to be doing to *live up to* the name "Believer." Even children have opinions on how a Christian should live, and non-believers will gladly tell you when they think you're not living up to the title.

While attempting those things, believers often act like construction workers. A lot of times when I was building or remodeling I'd have to force something into place. If it was wood, no matter how warped, I could usually do it myself. Sometimes I'd need a co-worker to hang on one end of a board until it aligned enough to nail or screw it into place. But I could do it—I was strong enough. And if it came out looking bad, wood-putty or wall-board and mud could set things right—or at least cover the mistakes. But up against a steel beam you find out fast that your strength is not enough. Even your friends cannot help. Regardless of how much putty you have on hand, you're not going to hide this. Manpower is not enough. If you don't have a power tool, you'll have to quit.

I started calling myself a believer when I was twenty years old and I thought I did pretty good at living like a Christian, for a short time. When I put my back into it, and when things went my way, I did okay—sometimes and compared to my friends. But it kept getting harder.

When I asked friends for prayer, they confessed that they did the same sinful things, over and over again. Like wrenching at what was warped and packing on the putty, we tried to force things to line up—and to conceal when they didn't. But knowing other lousy Christians was not comforting, and the list of things I had to hide about myself kept growing longer. I was trying to manhandle my warped *iron* will and I kept failing. Eventually I gave up. I hoped my children would be able to do it. I didn't want them to go to hell—but I was pretty sure I would.

But in the year 2007 I finally stopped wrestling, wrenching, and hiding things. At last I listened to what God was saying: I had never laid down my life. Not really. I'd only laid down pieces—sometimes and in part. I had not given "me" up. I wanted to become *a better me.*

I had not been crucified with Christ, so I had not been resurrected.

For the first time, I really saw who I was—in light of God's awesome Holiness. There I was, floating face down in my self, rotten to the core and without hope. A lifeguard could not help me. I desperately needed a savior who could raise the dead.

At last I understood His answer to my spiritual bank-ruptcy: the whole gospel. I finally began letting Him transform me and could just honestly say: "Yes, I'm a believer." Glory to God, moment-by-moment, by the power of His grace, I even live like one now. Through a clear understanding of the gospel, I'd like to help you live the resurrection life God wants for you. But *spiritual truth* is only discerned *spiritually*—if the Spirit of God decides to reveal it to you. So before we begin, pray something like this:

> *Father in heaven, I am in desperate need—I fall way short of your glory (your character). Fill me with your Holy Spirit and give me understanding of your will and your Word.*
>
> *Thank you for giving me new life through the sacrifice of your son, Jesus. Empower me to do whatever you ask of me. I sur-render my own will to yours. Amen.*

A Good Foundation

". . . try to find out what the Lord wants you to do. Do not get drunk with wine, which will only ruin you; instead, be filled with the Spirit." Ephesians 5:17-18

Find out what the Lord wants you to do and be filled with the Holy Spirit—these are not optional and they go hand in hand. *Blueprints and power* are the necessary foundation for a life of faith. We might call the *Word of God* (the Bible) God's blueprints, and His Holy Spirit the power.

But some of us want to do as much as we possibly can before we read the directions or break out the power tools. We think, *This is just wood; I've got this! I'll make it fit!* (Or die trying?) But we're missing the point—if it doesn't quite fit, maybe it doesn't even belong there.

We constantly need the Word of God and the Holy Spirit's guidance and power—not only when we think something is *beyond our own abilities*.

However, not all church-going people try to find out what God's will is. They're not all filled with God's Holy Spirit. Maybe they're sincere. They might even be leaders in the church. But they're trying to do spiritual things without the Spirit. How can you see when this is the case? The evidence of God's Spirit (what the Bible calls the *fruit* of the Spirit) is not growing abundantly in their lives. They might try to act like Jesus, but their efforts are *fruitless.* They lack a proper foundation.

If we are not filled with the Holy Spirit (letting His fruit grow), we will just be natural people. That would be okay if humans were naturally good. But man is *naturally* sinful.

A Natural Man

> "Make a tree good and its fruit will be good, or make a tree bad and its fruit will be bad, for a tree is recognized by its fruit." Matthew 12:33

A natural man might try to follow Christ, but he'll fail. He'll grow fruit, but it will come from his own nature. The natural self, or "the flesh" is God's enemy and produces the opposite of God's fruit. Galatians 5:22-24 describes the fruit (evidence or manifestation) of God's Holy Spirit. But before we look there, let's read Galatians 5:19-21 to find out what comes from your very own human nature:

> "What human nature does is quite plain. It shows itself in immoral, filthy, and indecent actions; in worship of idols and witchcraft. People become enemies and they fight; they become jealous, angry, and ambitious. They separate into parties and groups; they're envious, get drunk, have orgies, and do other things like

these. I warn you now as I have before: those who do these things won't possess the Kingdom of God."

Does this sound like anybody you know? Continue this paragraph for a description of the fruit of God's Spirit:

"But the Spirit produces love, joy, peace, patience, kindness, goodness, faithfulness, humility, and self-control. There is no law against such things as these. And those who belong to Christ Jesus have put to death their human nature with all its passions and desires. The Spirit has given us life; he must also control our lives." Galatians 5:22-25

According to what we just read, what behavior, emotions and attitudes (fruit) come from our own human nature? What attitudes or fruit come from the Spirit of God? Do you see the fruit of the Holy Spirit growing in your life? Or are you more of a natural man, controlled by feelings and actions that stem from your human nature?

To produce God's fruit, we need a miracle. So we ask:

Give me your power, we pray. *Change me, Jesus! Take away all of my sinful urges and make me holy!* we cry out. Then we wait. We're watching for a *ZAP! ZING! KA-POW!* instant holiness. We wait and we wait. And we wait. When nothing happens, we're discouraged.

We still get angry. We still envy and lust. We're still human. *What went wrong?*

A Field of Thorns

Before constructing a new building, you first obtain a piece of property and prepare the site. The life of faith is not much different. After we're bought with the blood of Christ, He wants to clear the site and start building.

> ". . . You are God's field. You are also God's building." 1 Corinthians 3:9

> "Don't you know that your body is the temple of the Holy Spirit, who lives in you and who was given to you by God? You do not belong to yourselves but to God; he bought you for a price. So use your bodies for God's glory." 1 Corinthians 6:19

Take personal inventory to see how God's temple building project is coming along: Do love, joy, peace, patience, humility and kindness flow from you like living water, refreshing those around you? Or do you often stumble into anger, jealousy, lust and pride? If your life resembles human nature more than God's nature, perhaps you've wondered how much of the Holy Spirit you received when you believed the gospel. A lot of people discuss this. They often have opposing conclusions. But the answer is really simple. If we're asking how much of the Holy Spirit we received when we were saved, we're asking the wrong question. Instead we should ask:

"How much of me did the Holy Spirit receive when I became a believer?"

If there is not a harvest of His fruit in our lives, it usually means we did not give Him access to our fields. We prayed, *Make me holy, Jesus!* But every time He tried sifting through our dirt and pulling on our roots, we dug in deeper and *rebuked the devil*. When God's fruit grows in our lives, it's a miracle. But it doesn't happen just because we said some magic words.

A fruitful garden is evidence of a hard working gardener. When we're ready to give the Master Gardener full access to our whole being, we'll finally see His power producing His fruit in us.

Sifted and Uprooted

We are meant to be God's field and His building. But if we want to be fruitful and well-constructed, we must take the first step. We invite the Master Gardener to work in us by changing our response to uncomfortable,

painful or frustrating circumstances. He's tried working on us before—anytime we didn't get our own way
He was probably trying to engineer something good.
But we resisted. We need a new response. Try these
phrases for a change:

I surrender, Lord. I give up—have it your way. Not what I want, but whatever you want. Not my will, but yours. You know best.

"People will reap exactly what they sow.
If they sow in the field of their natural
desires, from it they will gather the harvest of death; if they sow in the field of the
Spirit, from the Spirit they will gather the
harvest of eternal life." Galatians 6:7b-9

Wrestling with the Boss

"If we live by the Spirit, let us also keep in
step with the Spirit." Galatians 5:25 ESV

"And keep in step with God's love, as you
wait for our Lord Jesus Christ to show
how kind he is by giving you eternal life."
Jude 1:21 CEV

Have you ever been on a jobsite with someone who
cannot take orders? Work production is seriously hin-

dered when the crew will not take orders. Sure, sometimes you end up working for a boss who does not know best, but that is not the case when God is your boss.

Guess what? If you're a believer, your boss's name is *always Jesus*— no matter where you work.

Learning to live in step with the Holy Spirit is not optional. Your faith journey will fail if you do not get this. Sometimes we just don't realize that God is in control. We're constantly fighting against someone or something. But He's in control of everything in our lives (good or bad), so we're really just fighting *against God.* We think we're resisting people or circumstances, but we're resisting His Holy Spirit.

The Savior is all-powerful and perfectly good. If we've given Him our life, then we'd better believe He's in control of the whole thing, no matter who *appears to be* causing us trouble. This is the correct response in all circumstances: *Let all the answers come from you, Lord. You are good, and you're in control. I'll be thankful regardless of the answer You give.*

Not only does God control everything that comes your way, He wants to control your responses to give you victory—through the indwelling presence of the Holy Spirit, who is part of the triune God.

Christ in you—this is the KEY to Christian life. Christ's Spirit wants to live inside you, empower and lead you. Without Him, you cannot serve God.

Playing with Fire

> ". . . be holy; without holiness no one will see the Lord. See to it that no one misses the grace of God . . . . Worship God acceptably with reverence and awe, for our God is a consuming fire." Hebrews 12:14b-15a, 28b-29a

The Holy Spirit wants to live in us and give us the power to keep in step—that's some amazing grace. We cannot do it without Him. But how many actually try to keep in step with the Spirit? Even some religious leaders do not seem to care what God's will is—or to care that He's a consuming fire who requires holiness. If the fruit of the Spirit (from Galatians 5) is the indicator, plenty of people are not giving God access to their fields either. So is it a *requirement,* or is it a *suggestion?*

> "And do not grieve the Holy Spirit of God, with whom you were sealed for the day of redemption." Ephesians 4:30 NIV

Look at the Scripture above: *Do not grieve the Holy Spirit.* To *grieve* means to make sad. Read that passage within the paragraphs it fits into (within its *context*) and you will come to this ending statement:

> "Let no one deceive you with empty words, for because of such things God's wrath comes on those who are disobedient. Therefore do not be partners with them." Ephesians 5:6-7 NIV

God's wrath comes on the disobedient because they made the Holy Spirit sad. Grieving the Holy Spirit is a really big deal, even though it might seem like *everyone else is doing it.* If you don't want to be deceived or be partner to those who are under God's wrath, continue reading Ephesians where the specific things that grieve the Holy Spirit are named, followed by a list of behaviors that show we're in step with the Spirit:

> "You were taught, with regard to your former way of life, to put off your old self, which is being corrupted by its deceitful desires; to be made new in the attitude of your minds; and to put on the new self, created to be like God in true righteousness and holiness. Therefore each of you must put off falsehood and speak truthfully to his neighbor . . . He who has been stealing must steal no longer . . . Do not let any unwholesome talk come out of your mouths . . . do not grieve the Holy Spirit . . . Get rid of all bitterness, rage and anger, brawling and slander, along with every form of malice. Be kind and

compassionate, forgiving each other . . . Be imitators of God . . . Live a life of love . . . There must not be even a hint of sexual immorality, or any kind of impurity, or of greed . . . Nor should there be obscenity, foolish talk or coarse joking . . . For of this you can be sure: No immoral, impure or greedy person—such a man is an idolater—has any inheritance in the kingdom of Christ and of God.

Be very careful, then, how you live . . . Be filled with the Spirit. Speak to one another with psalms, hymns and spiritual songs. Sing and make music in your heart to the Lord, always giving thanks to God the Father for everything, in the name of our Lord Jesus Christ. Submit to one another out of reverence for Christ." Excerpts from Ephesians 4:22-5:21 NIV

Be very careful how you live.

Lying, stealing, anger, immorality, greed, foolish talk, etc.—these make the Holy Spirit sad and are characteristics of our "old self." Galatians Chapter 5 lists similar behaviors and character traits. In 1 Thessalonians Chapter 5 we're told not to "quench" the Holy Spirit. This statement also falls within instructions to put off the old nature—reject every kind of evil—and to be sanctified as blameless children of the light. Let's look at another section of Scripture about actions that come from our own nature, and about God's response to them:

"The wrath of God is being revealed from heaven against all the godlessness and wickedness of men who suppress the truth by their wickedness . . . They neither glorified him as God nor gave thanks to him . . . Their foolish hearts were darkened . . . Therefore God gave them over in the sinful desires of their hearts to sexual impurity for the degrading of their bodies with one another . . . God gave them over to shameful lusts . . . Since they did not think it worthwhile to retain the knowledge of God, he gave them over to a depraved mind, to do what ought not to be done. They have become filled with every kind of wickedness, evil, greed and depravity. They are full of envy, murder, strife, deceit and malice. They are gossips, slanderers, God-haters, insolent, arrogant and boastful; they invent ways of doing evil; they disobey their parents; they are senseless, faithless, heartless, ruthless. Although they know God's righteous decree that those who do such things deserve death, they not only continue to do these very things but also approve of those who practice them . . . God will give to each person according to what he has done. To those who by persistence in doing good seek glory, honor and immortality, he will give eternal life. But for those who are self-seeking and who reject the truth and follow evil, there will be wrath and anger." Excerpts from Romans 1:18-2:8 NIV

A Man Under Control

> "To be controlled by human nature re-
> sults in death. To be controlled by the
> Spirit results in life and peace." Romans 8:9

Notice in Romans Chapters 1 and 2 that they did not want to be ruled by God's truth, so He gave them over to be controlled by their corrupt nature. If we do not let the Holy Spirit control us, we'll be controlled by our human nature, which results in wrath and death.

But only by the power of the Holy Spirit can we escape the control of our "old man"—and only to the degree that we allow the Spirit of Christ to control us.

> [Jesus said] ". . . Human power is of no
> use at all. The words I have spoken to you
> bring God's life-giving Spirit." ..."If you
> love me, you will keep my commands. And
> I will ask the Father, and he will give you
> another advocate to help you and be with
> you forever—the Spirit of truth." ... "I am
> the vine, and you are the branches. Those
> who remain in me, and I in them, will
> bear much fruit; for you can do nothing
> without me." John 6:63, 14:15-16, 15:5

Under the control of the Holy Spirit, we'll grow His fruit and receive life and peace. Jesus said that he had to go away so that He could send the Spirit to us. We can do nothing apart from Him. This does not mean we cannot do anything at all. It means we cannot do the things that please God.

Not only do we need the Spirit to enable us to please God, but we need Him to teach us and keep us from being deceived.

The Bible promises that false prophets and hypocritical liars will claim to be speaking for God—when they are not. Some tell lies in His name and others do weird things and blame the Holy Spirit, though He is not involved. But if we'll continually surrender to the Holy Spirit and stay in step with Him, He'll keep us from blindly following false spirits and deceivers.

Want the Spirit? Just Ask!

Jesus promised to give us the Holy Spirit if we will simply ask:

> "So I say to you: Ask and it will be given to you; seek and you will find; knock and the door will be opened to you. For everyone who asks receives; the one who seeks finds; and to the one who knocks, the door will be opened. Which of you fathers,

if your son asks for a fish, will give him a
snake instead? Or if he asks for an egg,
will give him a scorpion? If you then,
though you are evil, know how to give
good gifts to your children, how much
more will your Father in heaven give the
Holy Spirit to those who ask him!" Luke
11:9-13

Just ask, Jesus told us! The Bible is clear and simple on
this subject, but men tend to make things complicated
and there's a lot of confusion about the Holy Spirit.

Evidence of the Spirit

Scriptures teach that the *fruit* of the Holy Spirit and the
gifts of the Holy Spirit are both necessary in the life of
the believer and in the church (the Body of Christ). But
do you know the difference between spiritual fruit and
spiritual gifts?

Earlier, in the book of Galatians, we read that the *fruit*
of God's Holy Spirit is love, joy, peace, patience, kindness, goodness, faithfulness, humility, and self-control.
The *gifts* of the same Spirit (as described in Romans 12
and 1 Corinthians Chapters 12 through 14), are something else. According to Scripture, spiritual gifts are
supernatural abilities and talents that people were not
born with but received from the indwelling Holy Spirit
after they were believers. These are things like prophe-

sying, healing, speaking in strange tongues and having uncanny insight or divinely revealed knowledge. They also include less sensational gifts like leading, teaching, giving, showing mercy, serving, and being encouraging. Having a spiritual gift proves that, at some time, you believed the gospel.

But if a person hardens their heart against the Lord and lives a rebellious, hypocritical life, they may continue doing *spiritual-looking* things, mimicking the Spirit.

In the world today, and in the Bible, there are many examples of men and women who lived carnal or worldly lives—grieving God's Holy Spirit—but who appeared to have spiritual gifts. Many of them were *spiritual* leaders. Whether they were ever gifted or were just mimicking the gifts, one thing is clear: they were out of step with God's Holy Spirit. They were *sowing seeds in the field of their natural desires* and (from it) they were *gathering a harvest of death*. (Galatians 6:8) But they appeared to be spiritually gifted, so people falsely believed they were godly men and women.

These people have always plagued the church. Many of their false teachings are taught from the pulpit or in Bible colleges. They are the so-called *sacred* doctrines that control some denominations. Therefore, we need the Holy Spirit to teach us as we search the Scriptures.

We need Him to guide us into all truth and warn us when we're being lied to.

> [Jesus said] "But when he, the Spirit of truth, comes, he will guide you into all truth." John 16:13a

In 1 Corinthians Chapters 12 through 14 we see a list of spiritual gifts. Their purpose is to build up the Body of Christ. (Later on, read those chapters and ask God to explain them.) Their theme is summed up here:

> "Now to each one the manifestation of the Spirit is given for the common good." ... "If I speak in the tongues of men or of angels, but do not have love, I am only a resounding gong or a clanging cymbal. If I have the gift of prophecy and can fathom all mysteries and all knowledge, and if I have a faith that can move mountains, but do not have love, I am nothing. If I give all I possess to the poor and give over my body to hardship that I may boast, but do not have love, I gain nothing." 1 Corinthians 12:7, 13:1-3

As I mentioned, I started calling myself a believer when I was twenty years old. I was zealous and passionate. I was the guy who always raised his hands during worship and wept in the presence of God. I eagerly desired the gifts of the Spirit. But I refused to *get in step* with the Spirit, so there was no harvest of His fruit in my life.

Likewise, the book (or letter) of 1 Corinthians was written to a church full of people who eagerly desired spiritual gifts—but not for the "common good." The author calls them "carnal" or worldly. They lacked the fruit of God's love (evidence of a Spirit-ruled life). They could heal, prophesy, speak in tongues, and teach! But they were proud, angry, jealous, and driven by their lusts. Their lives were not marked by God's love, joy, peace, patience, kindness, goodness, faithfulness, humility and self-control. Therefore, they "were nothing" and their spiritual gift was worthless; it did not profit them at all. How can this be? Gifts are freely given, but fruit grows on healthy trees whose roots are in good soil. When a Holy God is living and ruling inside of a person, God's character (love) will increasingly overshadow their human nature.

Gifts and fruit are both evidence that the Holy Spirit has visited a person— but fruit is the evidence that He's still there.

True Colors

[Jesus said] "Watch out for false prophets. They come to you in sheep's clothing, but inwardly they are ferocious wolves. By their fruit you will recognize them. Do people pick grapes from thorn bushes, or figs from thistles? Likewise, every good tree bears good fruit, but a bad tree bears bad fruit. A good tree cannot bear bad fruit, and a bad tree cannot bear good fruit." Matthew 7:15-18 NIV

"My dear friends, do not believe all who claim to have the Spirit, but test them to find out if the spirit they have comes from God. For many false prophets have gone out everywhere." [Jesus said] "Whoever does what God wants is my brother, my sister, my mother." 1 John 4:1, Mark 3:35

Jesus said that those who *do what God wants* are His family.

Receiving the Holy Spirit is simple and God freely gives spiritual gifts—for the common good. But appearing to have a spiritual gift does not prove much. The proof is in whether or not we *do the will of God*.

As we see in the lives of the Corinthians, some people just need to be educated. But watching for God's fruit is important—sometimes there's more going on than a simple lack of understanding. Since ancient times, pirates often flew *friendly flags* on their ships (instead of displaying their true colors). Flying a false flag got them within close range of their potential targets. Spiritual pirates are no different, therefore, we're to *test the spirits* and *examine the lives* (fruit) of those who claim to be prophets or teachers of the gospel.

Conclusion

In the following chapters, we'll talk about these things in greater detail and I'll tell you more of my testimony. Begin now going to God humbly. You cannot live the life He planned for you without His power. Ask Him to fill you with His Holy Spirit.

Begin reading the book of Acts in the Bible. As you read, pray that God will explain things to you and draw you closer to His heart.

> "But the Spirit produces love, joy, peace, patience, kindness, goodness, faithfulness, humility, and self-control. There is no law against such things as these. And those who belong to Christ Jesus have put to death their human nature with all its passions and desires. The Spirit has given us life; he must also control our lives." Galatians 5:22-25

When you're ready to lay down your life—surrender all of it to Him—He'll raise you in new life. Instead of fighting for your rights, making excuses, defending yourself, and getting angry when things don't go your way, practice using these phrases:

I surrender, Lord. Have your way. Not what I want, but whatever you want. You know best.

Supernatural

It's been said that Jesus did not come to make *bad people good*, nor to make *good people better*. No, He came to bring dead people to life. Analogies are not perfect, but imagine the difference between a building that needs to be remodeled or updated and one that's so far gone it just needs to be torn down and rebuilt. That's how far we (naturally) fall short of God's design.

When Adam and Eve sinned in the garden, they died—spiritually. This is the human condition. The life of God (that He breathed into their nostrils) left them. What He wanted for them and their offspring became naturally impossible. From then on they reproduced spiritually dead people, after their own likeness.

So if we're spiritually dead, how can we live *in step with the Spirit?* I mentioned that we must lay down our lives to be resurrected. But maybe that's a vague concept, so I'll tell you a story: I began calling myself a Christian when I was twenty years old. I was in college then, and on the football team at the University of Arizona. I struggled with sin and eventually gave up (until the

Lord resurrected me years later). I mentioned all of this. But I did not tell you that my nickname was "Preacher" during those early years.

Before I was twenty-two I'd handed out thousands of Bible tracts and countless New Testaments; I fed and clothed the poor; I took the homeless home with me; I constantly witnessed to people on the streets or wherever I found them. I taught Bible studies; I led worship; I even gave up football for Jesus. The game had dominated my life since I was eight years old. Now it felt like an idol, so I gave it up. After that I often spent whole days reading my Bible or on my face praying—*literally on my face* before the Lord. I gave away most of my belongings, strapped on a backpack and set out to tell people about Jesus in response to a dream I'd had. I shared the gospel with countless strangers and led hundreds of them in the *sinner's prayer*.

My behavior looked super-spiritual, but it really was not unnatural. I was always bold, forceful and passionate. It worked well in sports—although I'd been criticized for hitting too hard in football and being too strong-willed to coach at times. Now, I was zealous, but my overpowering nature and confidence hindered my faith.

I was like the man Jesus healed whose eyes were not opened all the way. *I see men*, he said. *They look like trees walking around.*

I was in that uncertain place where belief meets faith. If you do not put down roots, you'll wither away.

> "Listen! Once there was a man who went out to sow corn . . . Some of it fell on rocky ground, where there was little soil. The seeds soon sprouted, because the soil wasn't deep. Then, when the sun came up, it burnt the young plants; and because the roots had not grown deep enough, the plants soon dried up. Some of the seed fell among thorn bushes, which grew up and choked the plants and they didn't produce any corn." Mark 4:3, 5-7

Waiting for the Spirit

After Jesus suffered and died on the cross (paying the penalty for our sin) he was buried. Three days later He rose from death. For the next forty days He appeared to many people. But for those few people who left everything to follow Him (Mark 10:28), Jesus came and made an incredible promise:

> "And when they came together, he gave them this order: 'Do not leave Jerusalem, but wait for the gift I told you about, the gift my Father promised. John baptized with water, but in a few days you will be baptized with the Holy Spirit.'" Acts 1:4-5

In a few days you'll be baptized with the Holy Spirit, Jesus said. The word He used means to *submerge*—as in marinate, swamp, saturate, or drown. The disciples did not ask, but I'll bet they wondered what He meant. Yet they did not question Him. Keep in mind that this was not just *Jesus as usual*—this was after He rose again. They watched Him be crucified, *give up His ghost,* and be buried. Now He was back, telling them to wait for something incomprehensible. So they just nodded. *Uh huh, okay, Lord. Sure, we'll wait.*

These were Jews; there were characters in their Old Testament history who were temporarily filled with the Spirit of God—they prophesied or did impossible things. So they probably got the concept, in part. But the experience was rare and most had not been permanently empowered or changed. After Gideon's awesome experience, he remained polygamous and clumsily led the nation into idolatry. Samson continued to be ruled by sinful lusts until the Spirit of God eventually left him. And after the Spirit of God left Saul for his disobedience, he was tormented by an evil spirit until he killed himself. As Jews, the disciples had heard of God's Spirit, but they really did not understand what was coming.

As a young man, I was like Samson and Saul. I shot up quickly, *on fire* for Jesus. I may have looked powerful, but I was weak. My foundation was faulty: I was controlled by my feelings, not by God's Spirit. When my emotions agreed, I followed hard after Jesus. But when my roller-coaster feelings took a detour, I followed just as hard in that direction—and afterward I begged God to forgive me for what I had "stumbled into," again. Like the disciples before Pentecost, I did not yet understand that I was not humanly capable of being *who and what* God wanted.

Full of the Spirit, Without Measure

Jesus was the first one Scripture described as *full of the Spirit "without measure."* The Spirit did not just come upon Him, He was totally saturated—moment-by-moment, daily, 24/7, 365 days each year etc. He literally did not do or say anything on His own.

> "For he whom God has sent [Jesus] utters the words of God, for he gives the Spirit without measure. The Father loves the Son and has given all things into his hand. Whoever believes in the Son has eternal life; whoever does not obey the Son shall not see life, but the wrath of God remains on him." John 3:34-36 ESV

Everything the Son did or said came from the Father. So of course no one had ever spoken like He did! The crowds were amazed and His enemies were dumbfounded. His disciples were ready to die for Him. *Where else would we go, Lord?* Peter said. *You alone have the words of life*. He was not exaggerating—read the passage above again.

Whoever does not obey Jesus shall not see life; the wrath of God remains on him.

And yet, Jesus told His disciples that it would be better for them if He went away—if He returned to the Father, the same Spirit that filled Him would come to them. So Jesus ascended to the Father, and they waited—probably asking each other, *What in the world?* They soon found out. If you've been reading the book of Acts, you might have come to this by now:

> "When the day of Pentecost came, all the believers were gathered together in one place. Suddenly there was a noise from the sky which sounded like a strong wind blowing, and it filled the whole house where they were sitting. Then they saw what looked like tongues of fire which spread out and touched each person there." Acts 2:1-3

Suddenly these same guys (who were selfishly ambitious, slow to understand and frequently terrified) became selfless, ingenious, bold and unshakeable. They went out into the streets testifying about Jesus and working miracles. Unlike some Old Testament characters (who experienced the Holy Spirit but then reverted back to their natural condition), these disciples were changed forever by Pentecost. They spent the rest of their lives setting the world on fire (so to speak).

However, it's only fair to admit that even in Old Testament days a few characters were filled and empowered by the Holy Spirit in a permanent way—Elijah and Elisha come to mind first. An encounter with the Holy Spirit can be eternally life-changing or momentary. The choice belongs to the person encountering God's Spirit.

Like I did in my early twenties, a lot of men encounter the Holy Spirit and the seed of God's Word. But if their soil is bad, or their foundation is faulty, there will not be lasting change no matter how much they *feel* like they love God. Emotion-based faith withers quickly. If they do not put down roots, they will not grow the fruit of God's Spirit: love, joy, peace, patience, kindness, goodness, faithfulness, humility, and self-control. Their faith will wilt and their spiritual gift will not profit them.

If they serve *in ministry* after their faith has withered, they'll lead a lot of people astray.

Mimicking the Holy Spirit

By the time I was 22 or so, my faith was withering. If I had to guess what hindered me most, I'd say pride. I brought Jesus into my life to make me a better person—

I knew I needed some improvement. But I did not believe I needed to be demolished and rebuilt.

A supernatural life is not about becoming a better me. It is about signing the *title deed* for "me" over to Christ.

I wish I had understood this when I was young. At first when I felt convicted by God of some sin, I confessed and asked for prayer. I repented and turned away from it. But almost from the start, I was too proud to confess anything except little things. Instead of humiliating myself, I vowed to try harder and do better. *I've got this! I'm strong enough.* But the supernatural power I'd felt at first, the strength to turn away from fleshly desires, had left me. I did not do better next time. I did worse. And again, I refused to confess.

Despite my passion and good works, I could not keep from sinning, no matter how hard I prayed or how much I read my Bible. So I focused on things I thought I *could do* — like street witnessing and teaching the Bible.

My group of Christian friends were all young believers. Instead of studying God's Word to find His *revealed will*, so we could submit to it, we often searched for hidden secrets and super powers. We were not looking for the ability to change or to consider others above ourselves — as God's Word commands us. We just wanted an emotional high and the power to command devils, heal disease and solve mysteries. Unfortunately, around this time I got engaged to a young woman from the Bible study I taught. For the sake of privacy, let's call her *Theresa*. She was ministry-minded, attractive, and talented—so I thought she'd fit into the call of God on my life. And everything went well, for a week or two. Then Theresa tried to help me see one of my shortcomings and I walked away from the relationship immediately.

If you have relational problems or you're trying to choose a spouse, learn from my mistakes. My response in human relationships exposed and illustrated the state of my relationship with Jesus.

I'm not saying Theresa was the right person for me. But my response was wrong and I blocked the work God wanted to do in me. I refused to be ashamed. Humility was uncomfortable. My "flesh" (my master) rejected it and I refused to die to my natural man so God could resurrect me and produce His fruit (for the glory of Christ) in me. I fought to preserve my pride and my natural man.

I was following Jesus in the power of my own passion (*for my own glory*). I tried to do spiritual things while refusing to submit to the Spirit. Therefore, *I was without the Spirit.*

Supernatural Love

Men cannot love as God loves if they try to do it themselves. The fruit of God's Holy Spirit is His supernatural, sacrificial love—and it is not an emotion. God is the only one who produces it—yet He requires us to display it! Are you following this? If you think this sounds like a set-up, you're right.

God's requirement sets us up to NEED HIS SPIRIT INSIDE OF US!

Handing out gospel tracts, street witnessing, feeding the poor, preaching, and giving up football do not require relationships with other people. It's easy to mimic *Christian behavior* when we can be impersonal. God does not even have to be *in the house* for these shows to go on. But it's much harder to fake it when people get close to us.

Relationships reveal character. If we lack sacrificial love (God's nature), people who get close to us will know.

Relational behavior reveals whether we're fig trees or thorn-bushes.

> "I may give away everything I have, and even give up my body to be burned—but if I have no love, this does me no good." 1 Corinthians 13:3

God's love is supernatural and sacrificial. *God is love. He is love, joy, peace, patience, kindness, goodness, faithfulness, humility, and self-control.* If He is on the throne inside of us, He will reveal His nature toward people who get close to us. They may not approve—many people are offended at Jesus' character and His Spirit—but if He approves, that's all that matters.

I'm not saying that we who are born as thorn-bushes should try harder to act like fig trees. God's character cannot be taught or learned. Human sweat won't grow the nature of God. Only the Holy Spirit—God—living and reigning in us (as we surrender) causes God's loving character to shine through us.

> [Jesus said] ". . . I am not trying to do what I want, but only what he who sent me wants." ... "I have come down from heaven to do not my own will but the will of him who sent me." John 5:30b, John 6:38

Jesus was full of God's Spirit, *without measure*. He was totally surrendered and submitted to God's Spirit and will. *Moment-by-moment, daily, 24/7, 365 days a year*, He only said and did the things He heard from the Father. This is how we're supposed to live. This is what it means to be a believer.

God does not force anyone to be saturated with and surrendered to His Holy Spirit. It's a continuous choice.

Red-Tagged

I once worked for a company that was building a super-sized grocery store. It was the middle of summer in Tucson, Arizona—*hot* doesn't really explain it. Everyone was glad to see the footing and stem-wall completed. Soon some walls would go up, which meant shade. But then the job was inspected and we were told the footing and stem-wall were four inches off. The project was red-tagged until the crew demolished all of the work.

Another time, on an apartment complex, we'd just finished the rough framing when the inspector came in and said the wood was bad. This was more than a few boards—it was an entire city block of condemned wood. Everything had to be torn down. I didn't lose any sleep over it, but I was not the owner of the company.

> "And when he [the Holy Spirit] comes, he will convict the world concerning sin and righteousness and judgment. . ." John 16:8 ESV

God speaks to us silently through His Holy Spirit. It's amazing that a perfect, Holy God wants to communicate with us. We do not deserve it. But if we understand what He's saying, our "flesh" will always be offended. Why? He's saying we are not good enough. He's pointing out our sin and incompetence, asking us to let all of our hard work go. He's red-tagging us. A "red tag" in construction means the structure cannot be inhabited in its current state. Spiritual matters are similar. We ask Him in, but when He comes, He looks around and hangs a red-tag on us. *This building cannot be inhabited in its current state,* He's saying. That really hurts if we're the owner of this mess.

God created us with a purpose. We find the most fulfillment walking in step with the Holy Spirit. He makes life beautiful. We have super powers. We can fathom mysteries, command devils, heal disease, and have peace regardless of circumstances. However, He faithfully convicts us of sin—and our sinful nature is offended. The *inspector* wants the old man torn down.

The Bible teaches that if you meet someone who claims to speak for God, but they approve, excuse, or practice *the deeds of the flesh (sin)*, you're being lied to. Sure a red-tag is offensive and depressing, especially if you feel like the owner of the property. Truth often hurts, but it's faithful. Expect God's will to be the opposite of what your natural man wants. Then you won't be shocked and confused when it happens.

God's nature is perfect; He is love. Man's nature is corrupt and selfish. How could our natural desires be anything but opposite?

The first time you suspect the Spirit is pointing you somewhere you do not want to go (or trying to touch something you're sensitive about), you have a choice. If you resist Him, you will probably know it. You might feel guilty or scared. I remember the feeling—my body would shake like I was freezing to death. At that moment you know you should repent and trust God's judgment. But if you harden your heart and push forward with your own plans, His silent voice grows quieter. The shaking stops.

If you make a habit of pushing forward with your own desires and ignoring the Spirit, eventually that still, small voice is impossible to hear. You've turned your back on the Holy Spirit and plugged your ears. Now you're spiritually deaf *and on the wrong path.* If you keep your fingers in your ears long enough, eventually He stops speaking and moves on. No, the Holy Spirit has not been silenced, but He has stopped speaking to *you.*

> "Be careful, then, and do not refuse to hear him who speaks. Those who refused to hear the one who gave the divine message on earth did not escape. How much less shall we escape, then, if we turn away from the one who speaks from heaven!"
> Hebrews 12:25

God knows we will meet Him at the crossroads many times, wishing we could take a different path. He does not fault us for that. Jesus Himself struggled with this in the garden of Gethsemane. But in the end He surrendered and said to the Father, *Nevertheless, not my will, but yours be done.* We are guilty if we obey our desires instead of obeying Him. If we keep ignoring His orders or refusing to repent when He shows us our sin, He will not only stop talking to us. He'll stop listening to us.

> "Saul answered, 'I am in great trouble! The Philistines are at war with me, and God has abandoned me. He doesn't answer me any more' . . . Samuel said, 'Why do you call me when the Lord has abandoned you and become your enemy? . . . You disobeyed the Lord's command.'" 1 Samuel 28:15b,16,18a

In the book of 1 Samuel we learn that King Saul was chosen by God and (at one time) filled and empowered by the Spirit. (Read the whole story some time.) God stopped listening to Saul because he disobeyed the Lord's command. As always, it was a matter of surrender, not of works. Saul certainly had good works—he even performed sacred duties that were not His.

But his refusal to surrender and obey revealed a heart of unbelief.

"These people come near to me with their mouth and honor me with their lips," the Lord said, "but their hearts are far from me." (Isaiah 29:13 NIV) Righteous works are a good thing, and studying Scripture is needful if we want to hear the Spirit (God's Holy Spirit always agrees with all of His Word, the Bible. This is how we determine if we are really hearing correctly). But we must also draw near to God with our hearts. If we refuse to walk in obedience, the conversation stops. From that point on, no matter how much we continue to pray, unless we're telling Him we're ready to repent and obey, we're talking to ourselves—and we're on our own. That's a scary place to be. To hear the Spirit and be heard by Him, we must keep our obedience up-to-date. Keep short accounts; repent and change your thinking right away. Don't wait.

> "I cried out to him with my mouth; his praise was on my tongue. If I had cherished sin in my heart, the Lord would not have listened; but God has surely listened and has heard my prayer." Psalm 66:17-19 NIV

> "For the Lord watches over the righteous and listens to their prayers; but he opposes those who do evil." 1 Peter 3:12

Read those passages again. The Lord listens to *whose* prayers? What happens if I *cherish sin in my heart?* God's Word is clear: He does not speak to everyone; He does not listen to the prayers of all people. Sure He hears everything, but He is attentive and responsive only to certain prayers.

Getting a Green-Tag

Maybe you think it's hopeless. You've blown it more than a few times, so you do not have a chance of being heard. That's a wrong conclusion. The Bible shows us people throughout time whom God declared righteous or who received His eager response to their prayers, though they were not perfect. They were not born less naturally sinful than you and I. But they all had something in common: they went to God with a *willing heart.*

Go to God humbly, ready to obey. If you're willing to surrender, He'll supply the power.

Does it seem like He ignores you when you pray? Then examine yourself: have you *cherished sin in your heart?* Have you quarreled with Him at a crossroads, refusing to give in? If so, your relationship broke down at that point.

If your obedience is not up-to-date, time will not heal this. Pretending there's nothing wrong will not repair the breach. Doing good works will not make it right. Like a plant trying to grow in bad soil, your faith will just grow weaker. Your boss's name is always Jesus, no matter where you work. You are meant to be God's field and building. Since He bought this thorny patch of ground with the blood of His precious Son, He has every right to run things His way. So if construction has stopped, you're probably refusing the necessary demolition and fighting the construction of something supernatural.

To restore communication and get a green-tag, return to where you resisted God's Spirit (revisit the subject etc.) and resume the old conversation— ready to surrender and obey.

"You, like your ancestors before you, have turned away from my laws and have not kept them. Turn back to me, and I will turn to you . . ." "'The Lord knows those who are his,' and 'All who say that they belong to the Lord must turn away from wrongdoing.'" Malachi 3:7a, 2 Timothy 2:19b

A State of Brokenness

"But if we confess our sins to God, he will keep his promise and do what is right; he will forgive us our sins and purify us from all our wrongdoing."
1 John 1:9

God won't force His Spirit or transformation on us. Allowing the Master to tear us down and build something new—for His glory—is a continuous choice, an attitude of trust and repentance. Repent means to have a complete turn-around and a change of mind—it results in a heart change and a change of actions. Repentance isn't a one-time or occasional thing. Our corrupt nature is the opposite of God's perfect nature, so we must always be ready to repent if our will opposes God's will. It helps to remember that I don't own this building. I was purchased with blood. I must not give myself permission to do anything outside of the will of the inspector—who is also the owner of this house.

I've often described the life of faith as "living in a state of repentance." But that might be confusing, so let me clarify. If you're a new believer, you will literally be living in a state of repentance as you see that many of your daily habits and attitudes are sinful. You used to be controlled by your sinful nature, now you must turn away from all of that. But what about after you're no longer a slave to sins that held you captive before? You still need an attitude of repentance—be ready to change your mind and direction if it doesn't align with Christ's—but this might be better described as *surrender* or *brokenness*.

We must live in a state of trusting surrender and brokenness.

I'm no horse expert, but when I was in my early thirties, I owned horses and learned a few things (the hard way). Wyatt was my first and he taught me the meaning of "green broke." Wyatt was a Thoroughbred *race horse reject* and he wasn't really broke, he was just green (inexperienced). Despite the bit and bridle, Wyatt was often out of control. Fortunately, I was a stuntman at the time—I was paid to pretend I'd been shot, then roll off the roof and land on the sandy street below. I was in really good shape, therefore (and by God's mercy) I didn't get hurt riding Wyatt. A friend of mine wasn't so fortunate. Riding Wyatt was an experience.

When it was my wife's turn to pick a horse she brought home a mature palomino Quarter Horse named Lady who was *dead broke* and *bombproof.* Riding that horse was like sitting in the cockpit of a jet airplane, staring at the controls, wondering what each one does. Lady responded immediately and flawlessly to commands that I didn't know and didn't even realize I had given.

You might choose a horse that's green broke, dead broke, or somewhere in between, but some people choose to ride mules. They usually say it's because a horse that trusts you will go almost anywhere you steer him—and that can be dangerous, depending on your terrain. A mule, on the other hand, has a mind of its own no matter how much training you give it. I've been told it's nearly impossible to take a mule into a situation it thinks is dangerous—it will refuse and find its own path. That's fine if you think your mule knows best and you're counting on his understanding to keep you both safe. But Scripture warns us not to be stubborn mules or like the horse who needs a bit and bridle to keep him under control—we do not know better than God.

> "Trust in the LORD with all your heart. Never rely on what you think you know. Remember the LORD in everything you do, and he will show you the right way."
> Proverbs 3:5-6

Trust God enough to surrender—even when you think He's putting you in danger. His thoughts are not our thoughts. His ways are higher than ours. Live in a state of brokenness—moment-by-moment, 24/7, 365 days a year. *You know best, Lord. Have your way.*

Taming the Beast

When I was a young man, I didn't understand what "sin" was. I didn't realize that selfish thoughts and attitudes were sin. I let my mind dwell on the angry, lustful, selfish thoughts that came from my corrupt nature—and sometimes from the Evil One. Then I wondered why the things growing in my heart and mind kept producing sinful actions. I wanted the Spirit to help me overcome outward sinful habits, but I didn't want Him to overcome my inward man. However, like the horses and mule in our example above, brokenness or taming happens *on the inside*—if our heart and mind are surrendered in trust, the body will follow. Here are a few verses on the subject. Take time to read these sections in context when you have time:

> ". . . We take every thought captive and make it obey Christ." 2 Corinthians 10:4

> "Let the wicked leave their way of life and change their way of thinking." Isaiah 55:7

> ". . . Let God transform you inwardly by a complete change of your mind.".... Romans 12:2b

> "You have been raised to life with Christ, so set your hearts on the things that are in heaven, where Christ sits on his throne at the right side of God. Keep your minds fixed on things there, not on things here on earth." Colossians 3:1-2

> ". . . fill your minds with those things that are good and that deserve praise".... Philippians 4:8a

The Bible instructs us to surrender our hearts and our thoughts (every one of them, moment-by-moment, daily) to the Lord. Only when our *inward beast* is under control will there be true outward change.

In many situations and on many days our thought-life will be a raging battle-field. But if we allow defeat on the inside, we'll soon have the same defeat outwardly. Pray like this as often as necessary:

Lord, if that thought came from my corrupt nature, please forgive me. If it came from the Evil One, rebuke him and protect me from his fiery darts.

Fill me with your Holy Spirit; give me your thoughts and your character.

An Open Book

". . . if you are about to offer your gift to God at the altar and there you remember that your brother has something against you, leave your gift there in front of the altar, go at once and make peace with your brother, and then come back and offer your gift to God." Matthew 5:23

When I was young, I went to God secretly asking for forgiveness for my outward displays of sin, but I wouldn't obey Him, so the deeper problem remained. I had broken relationships; I had offended or emotionally wounded people with my selfishness and outbursts of anger, and I had broken my promises and vows. But I refused to confess, ask for forgiveness, and try to make peace with the people I had hurt unless I felt relatively safe doing it. But the Bible says that if someone has something against me—and it's my fault because I sinned against them—I'm to get up off my knees. God will not accept my gift until I've made things right with my injured brother or sister. Go, confess and make peace. God will be waiting.

The person we injured may not forgive us or want to continue our relationship, but after we've repented and done what we could to make peace, God will empower us, giving us victory over sin—He'll purify us.

But some might ask: If I stole from my neighbor, and he hasn't noticed, won't my silence do more to *keep the peace* between us? Or if I've broken my marriage vows, but my spouse is unaware so our marriage is still intact—isn't that more peaceful for the children? If you ask such questions, you're missing the main point and not addressing the root problem: your selfish, unloving heart.

Deceiving people is the opposite of mending broken trust.

Confessing secret sin to the person we've wronged may not mend the relationship—but they have a right to make informed decisions about us. If they no longer want anything to do with us, we shouldn't blame them. Don't have secrets. Hiding sin only keeps you in chains and makes the pile of hurtful things grow.

> "You will never succeed in life if you try to hide your sins. Confess them and give them up; then God will show mercy to you." Proverbs 28:13

If you're unsure what to confess, ask the Spirit to show you the things you've done that injured others. Consult the Lord about everything. Listen for the Holy Spirit and respond. And remember: confession is an admission of *your* sin. It's not an opportunity to bring up the wrongs of others or the part they played. Don't blame or make excuses for why *you had to do what you did because they did what they did.* Just confess your own sin.

Honestly Ignorant

Only Jesus can free us from the control of our natural man, and only to the degree that we surrender to His Spirit. But what if we really don't know what He wants? If we are ignorant of God and His Word, a willing heart might only get us half-way.

> "The word of God is alive and active, sharper than any double-edged sword. It cuts all the way through, to where soul and spirit meet, to where joints and marrow come together. It judges the desires and thoughts of the heart." Hebrews 4:12

> "All Scripture is given by God. And all Scripture is useful for teaching and for showing people what is wrong in their lives. It is useful for correcting faults and teaching the right way to live." 2 Timothy 3:16 ERV

By the time I graduated from High School, I'd only read one book during my childhood: *Charlotte's Web*. Even after a couple of years of college, I still was not a reader. I was a quarterback and school was an opportunity to play football. So when I was nineteen or twenty years old and a friend handed me a Bible and asked me to read out loud, I laughed. *I don't read*, I said. *Yes you do*, he answered. Then he sat there, waiting. After a long, awkward silence, and since I could not think of any more arguments, I stumbled through a few verses, out loud. That moment changed my life.

If you're not consistently reading your Bible, start now.

Stumble as much as you need to. You do not even have to understand it—you just need to read it! God cannot reveal its meaning to you if you're not even hearing it.

Ignorance cannot be helped when you're a new believer. But it isn't meant to be permanent. We must grow in our knowledge of Him to grow in our faith. Seek Him with your whole heart, study His Word, and ask Him to place you in the center of His will. If that's really where you want to go, He'll make sure you get there. Read prayerfully through the following verses and then answer the questions :

> ". . . The Lord is with you when you are with him. If you seek him, he will be

found by you, but if you forsake him, he will forsake you." 2 Chronicles 15:2b

"And without faith it is impossible to please God, because anyone who comes to him must believe that he exists and that he rewards those who earnestly seek him." Hebrews 11:6

". . . The Lord searches every heart and understands every desire and every thought. If you seek him, he will be found by you; but if you forsake him, he will reject you forever." 1 Chronicles 28:9b

"We are witnesses to these things—we and the Holy Spirit, who is God's gift to those who obey him." Acts 5:32

"I remember you in my prayers and ask the God of our Lord Jesus Christ, the glorious Father, to give you the Spirit, who will make you wise and reveal God to you, so that you will know him." Ephesians 1:18

Answer these questions according to the Scriptures you just read:

When is the Lord with me? To come to God in faith I must believe what about Him? What might cause Him to reject me? Who does God give the gift of the Holy Spirit to? Who will the Spirit reveal to me?

Conclusion

A supernatural life is a life in union with Christ. It is not enough to do good works—we cannot please God with human effort. He is not trying to remodel our old house, but to clear the ground and create something that only He can imagine and accomplish—He's creating a dwelling place for Himself!

> "Don't you know that your body is the temple of the Holy Spirit, who lives in you and who was given to you by God? You do not belong to yourselves but to God; he bought you for a price. So use your bodies for God's glory." 1 Corinthians 6:19

If we diligently seek Him, we will find Him. If we ask, He will give us His Spirit. We must approach God through the blood of Christ and with the correct posture (one of surrender, moment-by-moment, every day). Remember, God doesn't force us to be saturated with and surrendered to His Holy Spirit. It is a continuous choice.

Surrender your heart and thoughts (each one, moment-by-moment, daily) to the Lord. When you allow Him to control your *inward beast,* the outward will follow.

When your thought-life is a raging battle-field, pray like this as often as necessary:

Lord, if that thought came from my corrupt nature, please forgive me. If it came from the Evil One, rebuke him and protect me from his fiery darts. Fill me with your Holy Spirit; give me your thoughts and your character—love, joy, peace, patience, gentleness, goodness, faithfulness, humility and self-control.

Have no secrets and don't allow defeat on the inside; take captive every thought that doesn't obey Christ. Allow His Spirit to empower you as you continue practicing these phrases:

I surrender, Lord. I give up—have it your way. Not what I want, but whatever you want. Not my will, but yours. You know best.

Jesus on the Cross

What is the power of the cross? Not the *purpose* of the cross, but what is its power—as in horsepower, intensity, density or *wattage?*

Is the cross like a 20-watt light bulb for you? Maybe 60-watt? Is it 100-watt? Or is it like a floodlight at the football stadium? The power of the cross is directly related to your need for the cross—your degree of sinfulness. But here's the hard part:

To grasp the power of the cross, you need to take inventory of your sin. Can you see it? Can you see *all* of it?

Throughout the ages, whenever men glimpsed God they were struck by one thing: His holiness. Terrified, they often fell face down as though dead. Isaiah Chapter Six, verse one says:

> "In the year King Uzziah died, I saw the Lord seated on a throne, high and exalted, and the train of his robe filled the temple." *Verses 2 - 4 describe the angels who sur-*

round God declaring His holiness. In verse five the prophet Isaiah responds:

> "'Woe to me!' I cried. 'I am ruined! For I am a man of unclean lips, and I live among a people of unclean lips, and my eyes have seen the King, the LORD Almighty.'" Isaiah 6:1, 5 NIV

If we have not been struck by God's terrifying holiness, we have not glimpsed Him yet. And until we view ourselves in light of His holiness, we have not seen ourselves either.

It took me many years and a lot of grace and mercy (on God's part) to see myself. When I finally did, I was shocked—and horrified.

Remember when I mentioned my very brief engagement to *Theresa?* I'll tell you more of that story because it does not have to be *your story*—you can learn from mine. When Theresa disagreed with me, I blamed it all on her—*she had a critical spirit.* I was wrong. I should have responded humbly. Regardless, I still do not think she and I were right for each other. It was just too easy to walk away from the relationship. And she never once questioned my decision. I don't think there were hard feelings, but we rarely talked again, even when attending the same church. Either way, not long after that I met Cheryl, who would become my wife. From the beginning, this was totally different. The two were about as opposite as you can get. Theresa was a lot like me, Cheryl was not. Not at all.

Starting when I was twenty years old, I was passionate about God. My pride and natural desires defeated me and eventually I gave up. But do not get the wrong idea—I stopped believing I could please God and I stopped trying to resist sin, but I never gave up church. And that was not the first time I'd called myself a believer.

I grew up on the east side of Tucson, Arizona as the youngest of five boys. We were raised Southern Baptist and I was baptized at eight years old. As a boy, I did not understand Christianity—when people asked me if I were a Christian I'd answer, "No, I'm Baptist." But I was serious about my religion for years. Theresa also came from a Christian home and grew up in church, on the same side of the city. By the time of our brief engagement, I was consumed with ministry, and Theresa traveled with a dance and drama ministry, performing across the country. Like me, Theresa was athletic, extroverted, laughed a lot, and had plenty of confidence.

But Cheryl grew up in rural Alaska in an unchurched, non-believing family. Some of the towns and villages she lived in did not have a single church. When I met her, she was nineteen years old and had only met a few religious people in her entire life. She was an atheist, a single mother, and a cocktail waitress. She was very serious, quiet and reserved.

I was driving down a busy city street in the middle of the night when I noticed Cheryl in the car beside me. I did a double-take and then started trying to get her attention. Sure, I was passionate about Jesus, but I was passionate about pretty much everything. I'd quarreled with a co-worker earlier and now my roller-coaster emotions were leading me in all the wrong directions— and my feelings were my master. I was in the wrong place, at the wrong time, with the wrong motives. I convinced Cheryl to pull over, and I was not street-witnessing.

But after she agreed to visit with me, I started trembling like I was freezing to death. I couldn't stop the shaking. God desires to create beauty and life in even the worst messes—His hand was so heavy upon me, even with my proverbial *fingers in my ears* and my eyes turned away from Jesus, I knew it was Him. The shivering, fear, and burning within me grew so strong, I finally prayed and asked God to forgive me. Then I surrendered and preached to this sweet-faced girl with the long dark hair and doubting expression. She sat there and smoked while I told her how God showed His love for her on the cross. I explained that she was a sinner and that she was separated from God and from the wonderful life He planned for her. She did not argue.

She didn't say anything at all. She just blew smoke out slowly over and over again. Before one cigarette went out, she'd light another.

I read many Scriptures, showing her that God had made a way for her to be forgiven of her sins and reconciled to Him through the sacrifice of His Son. I explained the *sinners prayer* and asked her if she'd like to ask Jesus to forgive her of her sins and bring her into a right relationship with God. She didn't answer; she just looked at me like I was crazy. She was probably right.

I went to her apartment the next day and read more Scriptures to her, while she lay by the pool in her bikini, smoking and looking at me like I was green. Finally she said she wanted me to leave. Right before I got in my car, she asked me a question: "Why did you *really* come here?"

"Because Jesus loves you," I replied, "and I do too."

She rolled her eyes, turned, and walked away.

But after I left that day, the Scriptures filled her mind. A few days later she began praying the sinners prayer, all alone—over and over again to be sure it took. Her spiritual eyes opened and she started repenting. She cleaned house, getting rid of anything she did not want God to see; she stopped drinking, cussing, gossiping and stealing; she changed careers and gave up boy-friends and smoking. Her family thought she'd joined a cult.

What is the power of the cross? It depends on the comprehension of the person encountering the cross. Cheryl's response to the cross was different than mine had been—it looked brighter to her. She felt completely unworthy, with nothing to offer. Once she realized God was real—and that He loved her and wanted to know Her—she was like the prophet who cried out *Woe is me! I'm undone—I'm unclean.* Like Paul on the road to Damascus, the light of the cross and the holiness of God terrified her. She fell down and surrendered. Even though my morality and lifestyle had been far worse, the cross had not looked as bright to me. I could not see God's holiness or my own darkness. I grew up in church. I had memorized the Scriptures. My thoughts, attitudes, and actions were straight out of Galatians 5:19-21 (the deeds of the flesh), but I thought I knew all about Jesus. I thought I had all of the answers.

It's been said that religion Is like a vaccine:

You get just enough to make you immune to catching the real thing.

This was true in my life for awhile.

Up to Code

Before you build, you should research the codes in your area—and if needed, get permits. If you're not building according to the code, you'll end up red-tagged. And if you do not even know the requirements, you're not prepared to build *up to code*. Spiritual matters are similar; we recognize our need for the cross only as we see our shortcomings—are we up to code or not?

As a young man, I was very religious. But I did not have the glorious new life the Bible spoke of—and I wasn't sure what to do about that. We cannot see sin clearly without also seeing God's holiness, and I needed God to heal my blind eyes.

To show us what sin and holiness are, the Almighty gave the *Law of Moses*. This Law shows us what God calls sin and what His idea of perfection is (the absence of sin). *(Romans 7:12: the Law is holy; the commandment is holy, right and good. Psalm 19:7 says the Law is perfect.)*

The Law shows us God's character, which is perfectly *holy*. The Law might look confusing, but Jesus cleared things up—He summed up the whole Law like this:

> "Jesus answered, 'Love the Lord your God with all your heart, with all your soul, and with all your mind.' This is the greatest and the most important command-

ment. The second most important commandment is like it: 'Love your neighbor as you love yourself.' The whole Law of Moses and the teachings of the prophets depend on these two commandments."
Matthew 22:37-40

Again in the books of Galatians and Matthew the whole Law is summed up. These summaries show us how far we fall short of keeping God's Law:

"For the whole Law is summed up in one commandment: 'Love your neighbor as you love yourself.'" Galatians 5:14

Jesus said, "In everything, do to others what you would have them do to you, for this sums up the Law and the Prophets."
Matthew 7:12 NIV

The whole Law is summed up as *loving God with our entire being and loving our neighbor as we love ourselves — doing for them whatever is in their best interest, just as we would want done for us.*

The Law is not fulfilled by *feeling* like we love God or *feeling* like we love others as much as we love ourselves, but in actually doing it.

This is what God requires. Now go and do it! *Ah, but we have a problem . . .* Do you remember reading about the fruit of God's nature vs. the fruit of our own nature? We are all born with a sinful nature. Because we're naturally corrupt and deceptive, not only are we incapable of fulfilling God's righteous requirements, we are easily fooled—by ourselves. We cannot always see when we're being selfish and unloving.

Love the Lord Your God

Do I really love God? His Word delivers the verdict:

> Jesus answered him, "Those who love me will obey my teaching. My Father will love them, and my Father and I will come to them and live with them. Those who do not love me do not obey my teaching."
> John 14:23-24a

> "These people come near to me with their mouth and honor me with their lips, but their hearts are far from me. Their worship of me is made up only of rules taught by men." Isaiah 29:13 NIV

> "We truly love God only when we obey him as we should, and then we know that we belong to him." 1 John 2:5 CEV

> Jesus said, "If you obey me, I will keep loving you, just as my Father keeps loving me, because I have obeyed him." John 15:10 CEV

> "I am now giving you the choice between life and death, between God's blessing and God's curse . . . Choose life. Love the LORD your God, obey him and be faithful to him . . ." Deuteronomy 30:19a, 20a

If we worship God with our mouths, but not with obedience, we do not love Him. If we follow only rules of men, we do not love God. His Word declares that we love Him only if we *obey Him*.

So how are you doing? Do you love God with your whole being?

As You Love Yourself

Do we love our neighbors as we love ourselves? Do we love our neighbor's children as we love our children? Wait, do we even love our own families? I do not mean do we *feel* like we love them, but do we actually love them according to God's definition?

> "Love is patient and kind; it is not jealous or conceited or proud; love is not ill-mannered or selfish or irritable; love does not keep a record of wrongs; love is not happy with evil, but is happy with the truth. Love never gives up; and its faith, hope, and patience never fail. Love is eternal." 1 Corinthians 13:4-8a

Jesus said, "The greatest way to show love for friends is to die for them. And you are my friends, if you obey me." John 15:13-14 CEV

Love is not selfish, proud or irritable etc. . . If I'm impatient and unkind with my family, friends and neighbors then it does not matter how much I say I love them. It does not matter how much I feel like I love them. If my actions do not prove love, my feelings have deceived me.

"Do not merely listen to the word, and so deceive yourselves. Do what it says." James 1:22 NIV

What does *self-love* look like?

Do I love my neighbor in the way that I love myself? When I was young, I sometimes thought I hated myself. I hated not living up to what I thought I could be, do, or have. And I had a bloated ego, so I thought I could be, do, and have much more than was realistic. But self-love does not mean being satisfied with my looks, my abilities, my character or my situation. Self-love just means thinking of *me*, wanting to give *me* what *me* wants.

Love is an action, so if I'm hungry, I feed myself. That's the loving thing to do. If I'm stressed out, I find ways to relax myself. If I'm grieved, I want comfort for myself. If I'm accused, I defend myself. If I'm tired, I let myself rest—unless pushing myself harder makes me feel proud or impresses others etc. Wanting to be proud of myself is self-love. Wanting people to praise me is self-love. I might be worried about my problems and depressed by my failings, but when I have an abundance of negative thoughts about myself, that's still self-love. If I did not love myself, I would not care about any of this.

If I hated myself, then I'd be happy when *myself* could not pay his bills, when he lost his job, or when his loved ones and friends turned against him. I would even be glad when myself was lost in sins.

If I hated myself, I'd rejoice when I suffered! *Ha! Serves you right!* I'd say.

You probably remember well the last time you lost sleep over your problems. You fed yourself. You made excuses for yourself. But when was the last time you lost sleep over your neighbor's troubles—or fed him, comforted him, and came to his defense? A lot of us would answer, *I don't even know my neighbor's name.*

Humans can act and feel very loving to those who we think will return the love. We can perform random acts of kindness for strangers who we won't have to be in a lasting relationship with. We can even do amazingly loving things to be appreciated. But under these circumstances, the Bible says we have selfish motives.

According to God's Word, it is not true love. "I'm doing this out of the kindness of my heart!" we say, making sure everyone notices. We will sometimes fool people and we'll often fool ourselves. But we'll never fool God. If we want to see our sin and motives, we need Him to show us.

Turbo-Powered Grace

When Cheryl heard and believed the gospel, she knew nothing of church or of Jesus. She just felt like she'd been pulled from a deep, dark pit. Immediately, when the Spirit red-tagged something in her life, she threw it away or abandoned it like it was on fire. She read through the Bible constantly, *looking for Jesus*—she wanted to *know Him and bring Him glory*. And she believed that by digesting His Word she'd somehow be miraculously transformed into His image. She'd never before desired to be a *good* person, but now she believed she was a *new creature, in Christ.* She expected the Spirit to fill her up, change her into what He desired, and to take her wherever He wanted her to go.

> "For sin shall not be your master, because you are not under law, but under grace."
> Romans 6:14 NIV

When she went through trials, she praised God, believing He was creating something glorious. During her first year as a believer, her only child—her two year old daughter—was diagnosed with cancer. A few months later her daughter died, but Cheryl's faith remained strong. In fact, it was even stronger.

She was attractive before, but after her conversion I thought she was irresistibly beautiful. No, she was not an ideal candidate for a ministry partner, but I could not stop thinking about her. I wanted to marry her *for me*, not for ministry. She was good for me. And when she pointed out my shortcomings, which was not very often, I still wanted to be near her. I'd throw a fit, but I would not leave.

Eventually Cheryl and I got married. We were involved in ministry for a short time after that. Incidentally, Theresa also got married, and we all attended church together for a time. Although I did not know him well, Theresa's husband reminded me of myself, or how I'd been earlier. After a year or two the couple moved away to start a church. But by the time I was 27, I'd dropped out of ministry and was stumbling through life—frustrated, miserable and with a lot of secrets.

I wish I could say I dropped out of ministry for noble reasons, because I knew I was living an unfaithful, hypocritical life. But it was probably just because I was driven by my emotions, and I did not feel excited or spiritual anymore. I felt defeated. Sometimes I blamed that on Cheryl. She was praying to become encouraging, but I sure did not feel it. She went everywhere with me without complaining, but I knew she was uncomfortable in crowds and that ruined it for me. When she helped me lead worship, she was scared and had to pray and rely on miracles. She was quiet, shy and serious. She did not fit in with my friends. She was not athletic and did not enjoy playing games. She didn't even think my jokes were funny. One time I pressured her into telling me what she thought of my preaching. *It's good*, she said. I wanted more, so she added, *Very good?* When that answer did not satisfy me, she chewed her lip and added, *Well, I really don't hear from God when you're the one preaching. Sorry.*

Not long after that, I stopped teaching the Bible and leading worship. In fact, I stopped reading my Bible altogether; I put my guitar away too.

I had not been able to overcome sin, and then I was told I was lousy at ministry. It made me angry, but I had tried my hardest. Sometimes I wondered if things would have been better if I had married someone more like me—someone outgoing and confident. I could not imagine life without Cheryl, but our differences only became more obvious with time. She stopped wanting to discuss the Scriptures with me, and I often had to go to church alone because she was exhausted and had a lot of pain in her legs. By this time she was home-schooling our children, plus adopting and taking care of foster children. She taught women's Bible studies sometimes and ran a support group for foster parents. It made sense that she'd be tired, but I still wondered sometimes if she was a hindrance to me.

Over the years I heard that Theresa and her husband had built a large and successful church. I'd dropped out of ministry, but I never stopped going to church. I was still passionate about theology—especially debates about Scripture. And I still felt strong emotions for Jesus, therefore I believed that I loved Him—but I was mastered by my sinful lusts, anger, and pride.

I tried to believe that things were fine between me and God. But my conscience disagreed.

Sometimes other people would tell me I was not okay. *You're not a loving person. If you really loved God, His love would be evident in your life,* they said.

Can't they see how many loving things I do!? I yelled to Cheryl when we were alone. *Of course I felt like punching them in the face! That's what they wanted, so they could say they were right! They were trying to make me sin!* After I was rebuked, I ranted and fumed to Cheryl for weeks—sometimes months. In her quiet, gentle way (which made me feel worse) she tried to encourage me without actually taking sides. That was not good enough. Eventually I got angry at her as well. *You're taking their side!* I shouted.

But most condemning of all were the Scriptures I had memorized. Yes, a few verses could be taken out of context to reassure me, but if I did not twist them and remove them from their context—and if I did not throw out a whole truck load of other Scriptures—the Bible told me I was not okay.

You are not going to inherit the kingdom of God, the Bible said.

The Man in the Mirror

> "Anyone who listens to the word but does not do what it says is like a man who looks at his face in a mirror, and, after looking at himself, goes away and immediately forgets what he looks like." James 1:23-24 NIV

So how much forgiveness do I need? And how much forgiveness do you require? When we're ready to know the truth about ourselves, we can ask the Lord to reveal it to us—and He will. But even if we do not ask, He's trying to show us. When you're put under pressure, whatever erupts comes straight from your heart.

> Then Jesus said: "What comes from your heart is what makes you unclean. Out of your heart come evil thoughts, vulgar deeds, stealing, murder, unfaithfulness in

marriage, greed, meanness, deceit, indecency, envy, insults, pride, and foolishness. All of these come from your heart, and they are what make you unfit to worship God." Mark 7:20-23 CEV

The Lord tests us to reveal our character—if you're under more pressure than you feel you can take, get ready to meet *the real you*. God is giving you an opportunity to let go of self-delusion and allow Him to change you. Read slowly through the following verses:

"Gold and silver are tested by fire, and a person's heart is tested by the LORD." ... "Fire tests gold and silver; a person's reputation can also be tested." Proverbs 17:3, 27:21

"And I will test the third that survives and will purify them as silver is purified by fire. I will test them as gold is tested. Then they will pray to me, and I will answer them.'" Zechariah 13:9a

"He will come to judge like one who refines and purifies silver. As a metalworker refines silver and gold, so the LORD's messenger will purify the priests, so that they will bring to the LORD the right kind of offerings." Malachi 3:3

According to these verses, what two things (about a man) might the Lord test? Fire can represent difficulties, trials, suffering and painful loss etc. What's the purpose of the fire?

Inspected and Found Wanting

Growing up, my father taught me many things. Some were great—he was a compassionate, generous, devoted father—but one of his lessons was flawed. My childhood was consumed with football and (from my teen years on) I was also serious about body-building. Dad had been an athlete and he coached me to always compare myself to the *best of the best.* It was not enough to be better than people my age, or people in my area—I was to keep working and striving until I was the best in the world. But this philosophy only works for one person—the guy who actually is the best, and then only for a few short years until someone better comes along.

The rest of us are not that good and never will be. But if we remain self-deluded, believing *we are that good* (despite growing evidence to the contrary), we end up frustrated and dissatisfied. We make excuses, blaming people or circumstances for stopping us from showing the world what we're really made of. I saw this in my father's life, and in my own. Unrealistic goals consumed my father's life and stole his joy. By the time I grew up, he rarely left his favorite chair. He hadn't gone as far as he thought he should have in sports. And as a Christian, he had not overcome his smoking and other weaknesses. So he sat in his chair, all day and most of the night, day after day, smoking. By no means was Dad the worst of the worst in anything he'd ever done. But none of that mattered. He was not the best of the best. And by the time I was 27 years old, I was well on my way to becoming a carbon-copy of my father.

Although Dad's advice could only result in failure and misery, the concept (when applied to spiritual matters) is not that far from the truth.

The Bible tells us we are foolish if we compare ourselves with each other. Jesus is our example. He is the rule we are measured by.

A heart shape is often used to indicate love, but the cross is the true symbol of love. Our hearts are tossed one way and then the other. They can be deceitfully wicked. But the cross is an unchanging display of total, genuine commitment—in other words: LOVE.

> "But God has shown us how much he loves us—it was while we were still sinners that Christ died for us!" Romans 5:8

> "For Christ died for sins once and for all, a good man on behalf of sinners, in order to lead you to God. He was put to death physically, but made alive spiritually." 1 Peter 3:18

When I see what love is through Christ's sacrifice for me (while I was yet a sinner) I see my own inability to love. I cannot perform up to His standard—and it's *my fault*. But instead of giving up or living in self-delusion (blaming our failure on circumstances or other people), this revelation should bring us trembling to the cross. Yet not only to the cross (the crucifixion alone equals nothing but death), but also to the empty tomb and the *risen* savior.

We must come to the cross *and* the resurrection—to a grace powerful enough to both raise Christ from the grave and to transform me into His glorious image.

Conclusion

The power of Jesus' death and resurrection in my life is only as strong as I perceive it to be. If I fail to see my sin, and I fail to see God's holiness, I'll fail to experience the power of the cross and the resurrection. I'll treat Christ's death as a cheap thing. Yes, I need the cross, but first I must know my need.

You'll do well to avoid these phrases:

It's not my fault.
I was just...
I was only...

Practice these instead:

**It is my fault.
I am my problem.
The cross and the resurrection
are my only hope.**

Me on the Cross

It's been said that our mission in life is to enjoy our relationship with Jesus. But if that's all there is, we might as well go to heaven now! No, God has a purpose for leaving us in a dark and twisted world after He saves us—a world currently under the control of the devil. We're here to bring God glory.

> "Do everything without complaining or arguing, so that you may be innocent and pure as God's perfect children, who live in a world of corrupt and sinful people. You must shine among them like stars lighting up the sky, as you offer them the message of life." Philippians 2:15-16

The entire reason I exist is to bring God glory.

God saved me and is sanctifying me so I'll shine with His message of life—*and bring Him glory.* But we are not good enough to bring God glory. In fact, we cannot even have an intimate relationship with Jesus on our own. Our spiritual enemies—the devil and demonic powers—will work together with our corrupt nature to get in the way. However, you can bring God glory—not with effort and sweat, but as a brand new creature with the ultimate power tool: *Christ in you.*

A Strange Proposal

"... the secret is that Christ is in you, which means that you will share in the glory of God ..." Colossians 1:27-28

"For this cause shall a man leave his father and mother, and shall be joined unto his wife, and the two shall be one flesh. This is a great mystery: but I speak concerning Christ and the church." Ephesians 5:31-32

Christ and the church—a married couple? This concept will always be a mystery for many people. It's simple, once you get it, but it's *spiritually veiled*—hidden by God from earthly minds. You will not get it unless He reveals it to you. Say this prayer with me before we talk about it:

Dear Jesus, I desperately need your help to understand the mystery of new life. If I am under the power of anything (or anyone) other than You, please set me free.

Amen.

Christ in me, this is the secret of the gospel. This is amazing grace, the glory of God being shared with me and through me.

The Bible is clear that the union between the church and Christ is not "similar to" marriage—it's an actual marriage covenant. So to understand our new life, it helps to first understand marriage _as God designed it._

God created marriage with strict guidelines. He desires to use human marriage to illustrate Christ's relationship with His bride, the church. Marriage is not a friendship. It's not a business agreement. It's a sacred covenant between one man and one woman. Whether or not humans treat marriage covenants as binding and sacred, God does. It's wise to try and understand His design. Let's start at the beginning. Many people remember repeating a poem like this on their wedding day:

> "I, ____, take you, ____, to be my wife (or husband), to have and to hold from this day forward, for better, for worse, for richer, for poorer, in sickness and in health, to love and cherish, till death do us part, according to God's holy law, and this is my solemn vow."

They also answered questions like this, which the officiating minister asked them:

> "Do you take this woman as your wedded wife, to live together after God's ordinance in the holy estate of matrimony? Will you love her, comfort her, honor, and keep her, in sickness and in health; and, forsaking all others, keep yourself only unto her, so long as you both shall live?"

If you're married, you repeated the first and said "I do" to the second. But hopefully you caught my mistake above. This was not a *poem.* You took a solemn vow, binding until death!

God's design for human marriage includes a sacred covenant. His relationship with His church, the bride of Christ, also includes a covenant:

> Jesus said . . . "this is my blood, which seals God's covenant, my blood poured out for many for the forgiveness of sins."
> Matthew 26:28

> "Come, and I will show you the Bride, the wife of the Lamb." Revelation 21:9b

To have, to hold, to cherish, to forsake all others . . .

God's design is for something beautiful, nourishing, and holy. But your covenants, the one with Christ as well as a human marriage covenant, have two very real enemies. We've already discussed our natural man—he's an enemy to everything beautiful and holy. Now let's consider Satan. The Bible reveals that we're embroiled in a catastrophic world war—an all out battle between the forces of good and evil. Good will ultimately prevail, but for now we live within a war zone.

> "Be alert, be on watch! Your enemy, the Devil, roams around like a roaring lion, looking for someone to devour. Be firm in your faith and resist him. . ." 1 Peter 5:8-9a

> ". . . we belong to God even though the whole world is under the rule of the Evil One." 1 John 5:19

If you're married, I guarantee Satan will prowl your home, licking his lips. If he succeeds in devouring your family, it will not be because you forgot to pick up your socks and close the toilet seat—or you did not buy enough flowers or have *date-nights.* Your enemy simply has to destroy the living and life-giving core of your family: the marriage covenant.

Your natural man is another enemy of God and of holy covenants. Satan has an ally inside you; your natural self enjoys the evil darts his snipers shoot into your mind. But if you do not take these thoughts captive and make them obey Christ, you're in trouble.

> . . . "we pull down every proud obstacle that is raised against the knowledge of God; we take every thought captive and make it obey Christ." 2 Corinthians 10:5

James 4:7 tells us we must *submit to God* in order to resist the devil. If we surrender to God, the devil will flee.

But if we surrender to our own lusts and feelings (or to Satan's thoughts), we are throwing the gate wide open. If we open the gate, our soul's enemy floods us with temptations until we break our covenant: *mission accomplished!* Without a miracle, our family is sunk. The core of the family has been vaporized.

> "He who troubles his own house shall inherit the wind. . ." "For they sow the wind, and they reap the whirlwind . . . "
> Proverbs 11:29a, Hosea 8:7 MKJV

Demonic powers make an identical assault upon the covenant between you and Christ. Often the same exact fiery darts and temptations are intended to destroy *both covenants.* Does that make sense?

Maybe this is a good time for me to tell you more of my testimony: As a young man, my behavior may have looked super-spiritual, but I'd never been meek or mild. I was extremely zealous, yet passion was part of my nature. I was a blind man Jesus wanted to heal—but I needed another touch. *I see men. They look like trees walking around.* Unfortunately, I would not let Him touch anything I was sensitive about. I was in that place where belief and faith meet. When the sun and weeds came up, my faith withered.

> "Listen! Once there was a man who went out to sow corn . . . Some of it fell on rocky ground, where there was little soil. The seeds soon sprouted, because the soil wasn't deep. Then, when the sun came up, it burnt the young plants; and because the roots had not grown deep enough, the plants soon dried up. Some of the seed fell among thorn bushes, which grew up and choked the plants and they didn't produce any corn." Mark 4:3, 5-7

As the years went by, I often wished I were a better father and husband (and a better Christian), but my faith was very weak. I'd stopped believing I could please God or resist sin years earlier. I was angry at myself for this, but it was hopeless.

I was a proud, miserable, angry, religious man. I knew the Scriptures; I knew that my sin had separated me from God.

When I confided in people, telling them I thought I was missing something, they reassured me and said that I was fine. But deep down, I knew that I was not. Cheryl's father had a saying that applied to me: *Never encourage a man to climb higher if he's unsure. Send somebody else.* As a pipe fitter and welder, he'd spent a lifetime working on high-rise buildings. He'd seen men fall. "Trust the man's opinion of himself," he always said. "He knows himself better than you do." Likewise, I was convinced that I deserved hell.

My feelings were my *lord and master*, and I was overcome with despair. Early in the year 2007 I finally reached the end of myself—literally. One morning I left home in an ambulance before the sun came up. I was abandoning my wife and leaving my children a legacy of hypocrisy and suicide. But facing death, I finally humbled myself. I cried out to Jesus, begging Him to have mercy on me and give me one more chance.

At last I was ready to let Him demolish anything in me that made me uninhabitable—anything at all.

From this position, I finally glimpsed who Jesus really is. For the first time, I was aware of His awesome, terrifying, breathtaking holiness. In light of HIM, I finally saw myself clearly, and I was not proud of what I saw. I was disgusted, ashamed and scared. I suddenly understood the Scriptures I'd memorized. Jesus offered forgiveness and freedom from myself, in exchange for me laying down my life and accepting His new life.

Choose life, He said—*MY life, inside of you.* I accepted with my whole heart.

In His mercy, God healed me during my ride in the ambulance. The effects of overdose (which were rapidly advancing) suddenly retreated—though I had not yet received treatment. When I reached the hospital, I was examined and released. God had answered my cry—and now I knew what He was asking. I had to return to where I'd shut down on Him many years earlier. I had refused to confess my sins to those I sinned against. Specifically, I had not wanted to lose Cheryl . . . she wouldn't want me anymore if she really knew me.

But dead men have nothing to lose.

I had now given my life away to Christ—in exchange for His life that He gave for me. So when Cheryl came to the hospital to get me, I immediately began confessing my unfaithfulness, knowing I was about to lose someone I did not know how to live without.

A few days later, my wife—the best friend I had ever had—asked me to leave. She dropped me off at the airport, then drove away.

I was crushed, but I felt reborn. Everything looked new and different. I was beginning to see things as they really are, as God sees them. After glimpsing the holiness of God, I viewed my past with incredible grief and fear. I was so thankful I had not continued trying to be a spiritual leader when I had been a slave to my lust, anger, and pride. Now Christ began teaching me how to deny myself, to take up my cross, and to follow him—in His strength. Finally, it was not *all about me*. In fact, it was not about me at all. I had finally joined Jesus on the cross. Now the same power that raised Him from the grave had raised me—and was living through me.

At last I understood the mystery of the gospel: *Christ in me!* From that time on, I began cooperating with circumstances that He orchestrated to demolish my old man. As I surrendered to Christ, His character began overshadowing mine. My *natural man* wanted to argue or complain about each choice—and it will for as long as I inhabit this body—but as I surrendered to God, I watched the devil lose his grip on me and retreat (to return again at *a more opportune time*). Christ purified my heart by faith and every day became a miracle as He enabled me to live for His plans, His pleasure, and His glory.

> "God opposes the proud, but gives grace to the humble." James 4:6b ESV

> "And He has made you alive, who were once dead in trespasses and sins. . ." Ephesians 2:1 MKJV

The Bride of Christ

What do you see when you look in the mirror? A saint or a sinner? In what do you find your identity? Are you a brain or a brawn? The bad boy? The class-clown? The addict or abused child? Or maybe you're the star athlete? Who do you see when you examine yourself? If you do not see a dead man who was crucified with Christ and raised as a new person, (the *Bride of Christ*, in whom His Spirit lives and rules), you're probably still missing it.

Who do you envision when you look to Jesus? Revelation 19 tells us that when we see Jesus, He will not be hanging on a cross. He will not be riding on a donkey's colt, nor wearing a crown of thorns. When He returns to claim His bride, this is what we'll see:

> "I saw heaven standing open and there before me was a white horse, whose rider is called Faithful and True. With justice he judges and makes war. His eyes are like blazing fire, and on his head are many crowns. He has a name written on him that no one but he himself knows. He is dressed in a robe dipped in blood, and his name is the Word of God. The armies of heaven were following him, riding on white horses and dressed in fine linen, white and clean. Out of his mouth comes a sharp sword with which to strike down the nations. He will rule them with an iron scepter. He treads the winepress of the fury of the wrath of God Almighty. On his robe and on his thigh he has this name written: 'KING OF KINGS AND LORD OF LORDS.'"
> Revelation 19:11-16 NIV

This is not how our ungodly society views Him. But Scripture says this whole world is under the control of the Evil One—*the Father of Lies.* For this reason, if we try to learn about Christ, or about Christianity, from the world, we're following blind guides. We need to learn about Christ and about His bride from His Word:

> "Then I heard what sounded like a great multitude, like the roar of rushing waters and like loud peals of thunder, shouting: 'Hallelujah! For our Lord God Almighty reigns. Let us rejoice and be glad and give him glory! For the wedding of the Lamb has come and his bride has made herself ready. Fine linen, bright and clean, was given her to wear.' (Fine linen stands for the righteous acts of the saints.)" Revelation 19:6-8 NIV

The bride of Christ (in the verse above) made herself ready for the wedding; she was given "righteous acts" to wear. In the past she was dead because of disobedience and sins, but now she must be dressed with righteous acts—fine linen, bright and clean. And the bridegroom is awesome and intimidating, to say the least. If you've begun to realize that you do not measure up, He has a solution—but it's only for those who admit they need help.

> "You say, 'I am rich and well off; I have all I need.' But you do not know how miserable and pitiful you are! You are

poor, naked, and blind. I advise you, then, to buy gold from me, pure gold, in order to be rich. Buy also white clothing to dress yourself and cover up your shameful nakedness. Buy also some ointment to put on your eyes, so that you may see. I rebuke and punish all whom I love. Be in earnest, then, and turn from your sins."
Revelation 3:17-19

He rebukes and punishes all whom He loves? I must be earnest and turn from my sins? I need gold and white clothing? I'm pitiful and shameful?!

Yes.

The message is simple, but it's not easy. You may have heard a song (or a sermon) that claimed you don't need to do anything except receive Christ. You cannot clean yourself up. Simply believe in Jesus; *God accepts you just as you are.*

That's true, but it's only half of the gospel—and a half-truth is usually a lie.

Here's an example of how modern church culture often presents the Bridegroom, with Scripture to back it up:

"For God has said, 'I will never leave you; I will never abandon you.' Let us be bold, then, and say: 'The Lord is my helper, I will not be afraid.'" Hebrews 13:5b-6a NIV

This is a popular, encouraging promise. We sing it in church. We console each other by repeating it. When people are miserable or ashamed of their sin, they fall back on this verse. *God is with me! He's my helper! He loves me unconditionally!*

We know this does not mean God wants us to keep on sailing down a sewage-filled canal. But if we believe in Jesus and we're trying not to sin, then we're accepted, even if we lack righteous acts. *Right?* In other words, Do I really need *wedding clothes?* Do I need to cover my shameful nakedness? And is nakedness even shameful anymore?

Regarding the Scripture above, have you read that verse in context? It fits into its context like this:

> "Marriage is to be honored by all, and husbands and wives must be faithful to each other. God will judge those who are immoral and those who commit adultery. Keep your lives free from the love of money, and be satisfied with what you have. For God has said, 'I will never leave you; I will never abandon you.'" Hebrews 13:4-5 NIV

Read Ephesians 5:32 again:

> "This is a great mystery: but I speak concerning Christ and the church."

A Touch of Context

Context explains the verse and opens blind eyes—*the Bible explains the Bible.* That sweet promise is set within another promise (that God will judge us for immorality) and a warning that we must not love money, but be satisfied with what we have. The context is judgment and a warning not to love money (elsewhere described as idolatry or adultery against God.) Within the context, this concerns Christ and His bride, the church. Yes, He promises His bride that He'll never abandon her—but at the same time, He warns her to be faithful. She should not arrive at the wedding of the Lamb naked, filthy, blind—or *compromised.*

> "So the servants went out into the streets and gathered all the people they could find, good and bad alike; and the wedding hall was filled with people. The king went in to look at the guests and saw a man who was not wearing wedding clothes. 'Friend, how did you get in here without wedding clothes?' the king asked him. But the man said nothing. Then the king told the servants, 'Tie him up hand and foot, and throw him outside in the dark. There he will cry and gnash his teeth.' And Jesus concluded, 'Many are invited, but few are chosen.'" Matthew 22:10-14
> "Study to show thyself approved unto God, a workman that has nothing to be

ashamed of, rightly dividing the word of truth." 2 Timothy 2:15 JUB

There are many false messages and blind guides. We must study God's Word or we'll be deceived and ashamed—and we might not recognize the *real* Jesus.

To understand any concept or word, we need to see it in the context of the entire Bible. The Bible explains the Bible and verses are only understood within their context. So we find each time the word or concept appears in Scripture—this is called a "word study." If you're curious, wanting to know the context in which God promises not to leave His people, you can do a word-study on this. You'll find that each time the mention of God *never forsaking* people appears, it follows (or is followed by) warnings of what will happen if they turn away (forsake) Him: He'll forsake them; they'll be utterly destroyed. Here's an example from Deuteronomy 4:31:

> "For the LORD your God is a merciful God; he will not abandon or destroy you or forget the covenant with your ancestors, which he confirmed to them by oath."

That seems straightforward. God will not abandon His people. He's merciful. This makes a nice song or a wall plaque. It's very reassuring. But do not assume you know what He's saying until you read the passage in context. Ideally we should read the whole book, but let's just back up to verse 24:

> "For the LORD thy God is a consuming fire, a jealous God. After you have had children and grandchildren and have lived in the land a long time—if you then become corrupt and make any kind of idol, doing evil in the eyes of the LORD your God and arousing his anger, I call the heavens and the earth as witnesses against you this day that you will quickly perish from the land that you are crossing the Jordan to possess. You will not live there long but will certainly be destroyed. The LORD will scatter you among the peoples, and only a few of you will survive among the nations to which the LORD will drive you. There you will worship man-made gods of wood and stone, which cannot see or hear or eat or smell. But if from there you seek the LORD your God, you will find him if you seek him with all your heart and with all your soul. When you are in distress and all these things have happened to you, then in later days you will return to the LORD your God and obey him. For the LORD your God is a merciful God; he will not abandon or destroy you or forget the covenant with your ancestors, which he confirmed to them by oath." Deuteronomy 4:24-31

Notice that the context is marriage (again) and the theme is that God is a jealous God—a consuming fire.

In these passages the nation of Israel was His chosen bride and He warned them not to worship idols, which in other passages He called adultery. Although He ends with a promise of restoration (when the nation returns and obeys Him), remember it's the *nation* He has not abandoned. The individual men and women who forgot Him and worshiped idols have long since been destroyed; He's now dealing with their descendants. Here's another passage that declares God will not abandon His people:

> "Be strong and courageous. Do not be afraid or terrified because of them, for the LORD your God goes with you; he will never leave you nor forsake you." Deuteronomy 31:6

That is very encouraging. Drop down a few verses and the promise is repeated:

> "The LORD himself goes before you and will be with you; he will never leave you nor forsake you. Do not be afraid; do not be discouraged." Deuteronomy 31:8

Great! But what's the context? Keep reading; the passage finishes with this:

> "And the LORD said to Moses: 'You are
> going to rest with your fathers, and these
> people will soon prostitute themselves to
> the foreign gods of the land they are en-
> tering. They will forsake me and break the
> covenant I made with them. On that day I
> will become angry with them and forsake
> them; I will hide my face from them, and
> they will be destroyed. Many disasters
> and difficulties will come upon them, and
> on that day they will ask, "Have not these
> disasters come upon us because our God
> is not with us?" And I will certainly hide
> my face on that day because of all their
> wickedness in turning to other gods.'"
> Deuteronomy 31:16-18

Again, what is the context? A broken marriage covenant and a jealous husband whose bride has prostituted
herself, or committed adultery. Do you see the pattern?

Evidently, showing up to the wedding of the Lamb
filthy, blind, and naked is not a good idea—and this
Bridegroom expects faithfulness. He wants a bride who
is united to Him and brings Him glory, not shame.

If you want to continue the word-study we began, open
your Bible and answer some questions. (These use the
original NIV).

Joshua 24:20 says "if you forsake the LORD," He will
do WHAT? In 2 Kings 21:14-15 WHY will God forsake

and hand these people over to the enemy? According to 1 Chronicles 28:9 and 2 Chronicles 15:2 if you seek Him, He will be found by you; but if you forsake Him, WHAT will happen? In Ezra 8:22 WHO is God's great anger against? In Isaiah 1:28 WHAT will happen to those who forsake the LORD? In Jeremiah 23:16-17 WHAT do false prophets tell those who follow the stubbornness of their hearts? Is it true?

Christ: the Key

The Bible is clear: God is a jealous God who requires faithfulness, but we are naturally bent toward unfaithfulness. Even if we try to keep the Law with all of our strength, we will fail—just one violation or omission is the same as breaking the whole thing. Without Jesus inside my body, living His life through me, I produce only *deeds of the flesh*. But Christ is God's secret—He is the key. He does not just want to reveal Himself *to you*. He wants to reveal Himself *through you*. When you're united with Him, He will conform you into His glorious image.

> "In this way they will know God's secret, which is Christ himself. He is the key that opens all the hidden treasures of God's wisdom and knowledge." Colossians 2:2b-3

> "God's plan is to make known his secret to his people, this rich and glorious secret

which he has for all peoples. And the
secret is that Christ is in you, which
means that you will share in the glory of
God. So we preach Christ to everyone.
With all possible wisdom we warn and
teach them in order to bring each one into
God's presence as a mature individual in
union with Christ." Colossians 1:27-28

What does it mean to be *in union with Christ?* Christ
died for us while we were sinners; we get that. We
believe it. But a lot of people get stuck here—claiming
unity with Christ, but living separate lives, not realizing that *separation* is the opposite of *unity.* Since believing, they've changed a little bit; they now feel guilty
and try to hide their sin. Practically speaking, they're
just sinners in Sunday clothes—they can't trust Him
enough to surrender and obey. If this sounds like you,
how can you escape and finally have evidence of genuine faith?

How can you escape the power of the Law (which amounts to being mastered by your body) and be united with Christ—mastered by His Spirit? The answer is to die.

"For when we die, we are set free from the
power of sin. Since we have died with
Christ, we believe that we will also live
with him." Romans 6:7-8

Death?! Can't we just try harder to obey the Law? No—the Law was not created to improve anyone. The Law was given to officially certify (and reveal) our condemnation—not to provide salvation. However, we can escape the Law and condemnation. God provided just one way: *death and resurrection.* (Without a death, there can be no resurrection.) Read slowly through the following verses and see if you can answer the questions:

> "The law rules over people only as long as they live. A married woman, for example, is bound by the law to her husband as long as he lives; but if he dies, then she is free from the law that bound her to him. So then, if she lives with another man while her husband is alive, she will be called an adulteress; but if her husband dies, she is legally a free woman and does not commit adultery if she marries another man. That is how it is with you, my friends. As far as the Law is concerned, you also have died because you are part of the Body of Christ; and now you belong to him who was raised from death in order that we might be useful in the service of God. For when we lived according to our human nature, the sinful desires stirred up by the Law were at work in our bodies, and all we did ended in death." Romans 7:1-6

> "I have been crucified with Christ and I no longer live, but Christ lives in me. The

life I live in the body, I live by faith in the
Son of God, who loved me and gave him-
self for me. I do not set aside the grace of
God, for if righteousness could be gained
through the law, Christ died for nothing!"
Galatians 2:20-21

If I have not been (WHAT?) with Christ, then I'm still
living and He does not live in me. If (WHAT?) could be
gained through the Law, Christ died in vain. I was born
married to the Law; if I have not died with Christ, I'm
still (WHAT?). In that case, I cannot marry another
without committing (WHAT?).

Christ is holy. He will not commit adultery by uniting
Himself with someone who is not "free from the Law."
But the Bible says that if I have not been crucified, I'm
still "married" to the Law. And I cannot divorce the
Law, it's perfectly blameless. Galatians Chapter 5 tells
me that if I'm united with the Law, even if I try my best
to keep it, I'm separated from Christ:

"Those of you who try to be put right with
God by obeying the Law have cut yourselves off from Christ. You are outside
God's grace. As for us, our hope is that
God will put us right with him; and this
is what we wait for by the power of God's
Spirit working through our faith. For
when we are in union with Christ Jesus,
neither circumcision nor the lack of it
makes any difference at all; what matters

is faith that works through love." Excerpts from Galatians 5

Romans Chapters 6 and 7 teach that when I was married to the Law, we produced children. These children were "fruit to death"—in other words: sin. The Law produced sin in me, and I was married for life. Each time I went near the Law, trying to keep it, we produced another sin. But I was not free to leave. My covenant with the Law was unbreakable. The only legal way out of that covenant was for one of the partners to die. The Law will never die. That left just one option.

Dying to be Free

Me on the cross—this is the only way I could be resurrected and have Christ in me. Recently we read: "For when we die, we are set free from the power of sin. Since we have died with Christ, we believe that we will also live with him." (Romans 6:7-8) *If I died with Him, I shall also live with Him.* My death freed me from my former marriage to the Law. No longer does the Law produce offspring of death in me. I'm *dead to sin and alive to Christ*. I'm the bride of Christ, and this mysterious union, Christ in me, produces "fruit to God"—or righteousness: CLEAN, WHITE WEDDING CLOTHES!

What does this resurrected life look like? Read slowly through the following verses to see:

"You were set free from sin and became the slaves of righteousness." Romans 6:18

"You have been raised to life with Christ, so set your hearts on the things that are in heaven, where Christ sits on his throne at the right side of God. Keep your minds fixed on things there, not on things here on earth. For you have died, and your life is hidden with Christ in God. Your real life is Christ and when he appears, then you too will appear with him and share his glory! You must put to death, then, the earthly desires at work in you, such as sexual immorality, indecency, lust, evil passions, and greed (for greed is a form of idolatry). Because of such things God's anger will come upon those who do not obey him. At one time you yourselves used to live according to such desires, when your life was dominated by them. But now you must get rid of all these things: anger, passion, and hateful feelings. No insults or obscene talk must ever come from your lips. Do not lie to one another, for you have put off the old self with its habits and have put on the new self. This is the new being which God, its Creator, is constantly renewing in his own image, in order to bring you to a full knowledge of himself." Colossians 3:1-10

[Jesus said] "Remain united to me, and I will remain united to you. A branch can-

> not bear fruit by itself; it can do so only if
> it remains in the vine. In the same way
> you cannot bear fruit unless you remain
> in me." John 15:4

I am now a slave to righteousness. I must put to death the desires of my natural man—moment-by-moment, every day. The only path to union with Christ is through *death to self.* I have a supernatural, resurrected life. I have the Spirit of God inside of me. I have the mind of Christ. I am now seated in heavenly places! But wait—listen to this: As we live a resurrected life, we still feel the "earthly desires" that come from our flesh. Yes, you will still have thoughts that come from your old man or from the devil. The difference is that you finally have a CHOICE. You are *set free to choose.* Will you die constantly to your emotions, desires, and plans? Will you continually come alive to Christ's desires and plans? If you choose it, He'll enable you to do it.

The Holy Spirit in me teaches me God's will and then gives me the power to do it. He also gives me the desire to do His will.

> "For God is working in you, giving you the
> desire and the power to do what pleases
> him." Philippians 2:13 NLT

If I find myself struggling with sin, unable to do God's will, I am *out of step* with the Holy Spirit. Because His power is made perfect in weakness, if I'm suddenly powerless, it's my fault—I have been resisting Him.

God won't force me to trust Him and surrender to His Spirit—it's a continuous choice.

To get back in step with the Spirit, I must choose to die to myself in each decision. If I need to find my identity in me—my accomplishments, my attributes—I'm refusing to lay myself down. If I'm holding on to my plans, my desires, and my life, then I'm still under the Law—I am cut off from Christ and can produce only *fruit to death*.

But when I trust Him, surrendering to His Spirit within me, *moment-by-moment, all day, every day* (not only when I think I'm up against something beyond my own strength) I am united with Christ and filled with His power. God gives me His new life and conforms me into the glorious image of Christ.

> "We ask God to fill you with the knowledge of his will, with all the wisdom and understanding that his Spirit gives. Then you will be able to live as the Lord wants and will always do what pleases him. Your lives will produce all kinds of good deeds, and you will grow in your knowledge of God . . . He rescued us from the power of darkness and brought us safe

into the kingdom of his dear Son, by whom we are set free, that is, our sins are forgiven . . . At one time you were far away from God and were his enemies because of the evil things you did and thought. But now, by means of the physical death of his Son, God has made you his friends, in order to bring you, holy, pure, and faultless, into his presence. You must, of course, continue faithful on a firm and sure foundation, and must not allow yourselves to be shaken from the hope you gained when you heard the gospel. . . .God's plan is to make known his secret to his people, this rich and glorious secret which he has for all peoples. And the secret is that Christ is in you, which means that you will share in the glory of God." Excerpts from Colossians 1

Conclusion

After believing the gospel, God brings each man to a point where He asks him to choose: *Will you remain you? Or will you lay your self down, pick up your cross, and let me remake you in my image—for my glory?*

Will you give yourself permission to have a temper, because you're Irish? Will you see yourself as the addict or the unloved child? Will I still insist on finding my identity in being the star athlete? Or will I die to my old identity and tendencies? Will we lose ourselves and let God decide who we are?

Some of us are brought to this point over and over again. But if we refuse to be crucified, we cannot be raised in new life. If we resist the Spirit of God, we might still be religious. We might attend church, we might even preach and teach. But we'll be blind guides—Pharisees, and later (probably) Pharisee drop-outs. Keeping the Law on our own is impossible. The Law produces only death in us. But through our death, each moment and each decision, we allow God's Spirit to raise us up in His power, to live His new life for His glory. As I repent of me and surrender to Him—to Christ, who is my life—I'm empowered by this union and clothed in His righteousness.

Ask God to explain what it means to be *dead to sin and alive to Christ*. Ask Him to show you the power available to those who are crucified with Christ. Ask Him to help you to lay down your life and accept His new life within you. Ask Him to set you free from the power of your feelings, desires, and body, and to enable you to walk in the power of the Holy Spirit.

> "Don't you know that your body is the temple of the Holy Spirit, who lives in you and who was given to you by God? You do not belong to yourselves but to God; he bought you for a price. So use your bodies for God's glory." 1 Corinthians 6:19

Try these phrases for a change:

It's not about me. I no longer live, but Christ lives in me. When I surrender to God, the devil has to flee. My purpose in life is to bring God glory, with the strength He provides.

The Power of Grace

It's been said that Christians should not be known for what we stand *against*, but for what we stand *for*: **Jesus.** This sounds clever, but it does not work. We stand for Jesus by turning against whatever He hates—by the power of *Christ in us*.

> "To honor the LORD is to hate evil"... "Hate what is evil, hold on to what is good"... "You must turn away from evil and do good"... "Those who say they belong to the Lord must turn away from wrongdoing." Proverbs 8:13, Romans 12:9, 1 Peter 3:11, 2 Timothy 2:19

People who suddenly hate the evil they used to enjoy are noticeable. Very noticeable. The Word of the Lord spreads widely and grows in power through them.

> ". . . They were all seized with fear, and the name of the Lord Jesus was held in high honor. Many of those who believed now came and openly confessed their evil deeds. A number who had practiced sorcery brought their scrolls together and burned them publicly. . . . In this way the

word of the Lord spread widely and grew in power." Acts 19:17b-19a, 20 NIV

We bring God glory and honor by hating the things He hates. Also, Jesus said that the path to life is *narrow* and few will find it. But those two statements sound harsh—*and God is love.* We want people to know He's patient and kind. Maybe this is why many people spend more time preaching *against convictions* than they do preaching *against sin.* But this will not end well. Let me illustrate: In 2007, when I confessed my sins to Cheryl and was finally set free from the power of my self, she knew it was real. She had not known every bad thing about me, but she knew me well enough to know I was not capable of faking change or actually changing—and I'd just been radically transformed. Suddenly I loved the things God loves—*people*—and I hated things that he hated, such as my own nature and my pride. And yet, my past behavior had vaporized the core of our marriage, troubled our children, and devastated my wife.

> "He who troubles his own house shall inherit the wind. . ." "For they sow the wind, and they reap the whirlwind . . . "
> Proverbs 11:29a, Hosea 8:7 MKJV

When Cheryl told me to go, I left without a fight—I did not deserve to stay. But I was grieved and worried, and not just for myself. This was the first time Cheryl and I had separated in eighteen years. Because we had recently moved to a new state, we didn't know anyone within hundreds of miles. Now I was leaving her alone in the middle of winter, almost snowbound—miles from town—with a broken heart and a house full of children to take care of.

It was a really bad situation. All I could do was pray.

I've read that the late Billy Graham always had the same answer each time he was asked who the godliest Christian he'd ever met was: *My wife Ruth*, he'd say. I understand where he's coming from. But for many years I just did not get it. In fact, once when I was a young man I asked Cheryl, "What do you like?" We'd been married for years at that point, but I really didn't know. She was always doing things for me, or for our children—or for other needy people. I never saw her do anything solely for her own enjoyment. When she just stared at me, I added, "I'm not asking what you think is right or good or holy, or what you think God wants you to like," I said, "but what do *you personally* really like?"

She just looked at me, baffled. When I kept pressuring her for an answer, she finally said, "I have no idea. I'm a Christian."

"What's that supposed to mean," I asked, starting to get angry. Was she implying that I was not as good of a Christian!?

When she finally answered, I was the confused one. "I'm naturally sinful," she said. "I've been denying my *self* since I was nineteen years old. I haven't let my *self* tell me what it wants or likes since then, because I don't trust it. So, I just don't know."

Of course I knew we had sinful natures. I knew the Scriptures better than she did! And I was not so blind that I did not notice that her behavior was more Christian-like than mine. But I assumed that was because she'd started out as a good girl. After all, from the time I'd met her, excluding the first two days, she'd been sweet and pure.

The Delusion Fades

So what do you like, really? And who do you see when you look into the mirror? What's your *identity*? When you examine yourself, who do you find? I hope you see an ex-dead man who's now a resurrected slave of righteousness.

When Cheryl and I were young, people sometimes called her "legalistic." She rarely mentioned her convictions and she did not push them on people. But her attitude and lifestyle set her apart. She cared more about *His* opinion than she did about people's opinions, and yet, she considered other people better than herself. And she was more in love with Jesus than she was with me—this caused problems. She was a quiet, gentle, helpful, submissive wife—because the Bible told her to be—but she was intolerant and unyielding in matters of righteousness. With such strong convictions, she came across as opinionated and narrow-minded. My friends were nervous around her. Honestly, I was too. When people called her legalistic to her face, she'd just smile and roll her eyes. "You must not know me," she'd say. "I'm sure this is God's will. If this were my idea and my strength, I'd fail. I couldn't be a good girl if my life depended on it."

I did not understand her then, but now I get it. The person I was married to was not *natural*—she was filled with and surrendered to the Holy Spirit.

> "But the gate to life is narrow and the way that leads to it is hard, and there are few people who find it. Be on your guard against false prophets; they come to you looking like sheep on the outside, but on the inside they are really like wild wolves." Matthew 7:14-15

Narrow Minded People

That game-changing winter of 2007, after Cheryl sent me away, I spent three days either on the phone talking with her or on my face praying. Meanwhile, she went to Jesus and begged Him to show her what to do. Then on the fourth day, she let me come home.

As she continued to pray—begging for guidance and strength—she saw areas in her own life, and in our home, where my rebellion brought compromise into the family. In the book of Joshua when God's people were defeated, Joshua cried out in prayer and the Lord answered in essence: *Get up off your face! There's sin in the camp and you cannot stand until you remove these things.* After Joshua cleansed the camp, "the LORD was no longer furious." Likewise, Cheryl began cleaning house, purging her life and our home of anything that was not inviting to God's Spirit. She took drastic measures and received even more criticism, but the Evil One's influence on our family—his teeth-marks—began to fade.

My children needed their Dad and Cheryl needed a true friend. I prayed that God would help me repair the damage I'd done. A broken covenant cannot be taped back together, but we entered into a new covenant and a new life together. I began rising early each morning, looking for ways to serve my family and walking the perimeter of our property, begging the Spirit of God to purify us, and to invade our land, home, and hearts.

I was finally on the narrow path Cheryl had been walking on for years. I began realizing how merciful and kind God had been when He allowed me to find a wife who was more in love with Him than she was with me—that devotion saved us from unspeakable things.

Saved by Faith Alone

I've heard it said that grace and faith are static concepts that do not work. That idea is not biblically sound. If your faith and grace cannot move your mountains, open your blind eyes, and deliver your family from the lion's mouth, you're missing it. *You see men. They look like trees walking around.*

Keep asking, keep seeking—keep on knocking. Do not give up until you're fully healed.

In Matthew Chapter 15 a Canaanite woman fell at Jesus' feet, begging him to save her daughter from the power of a demon. She refused to leave Jesus until her daughter was set free. She sought Him stubbornly. She pursued Him persistently.

Jesus said she had *great faith*. If faith is a static *do-nothing* concept, how did Jesus measure her faith?

> "... through Jesus the forgiveness of sins is proclaimed to you. Through him everyone who believes is justified from everything you could not be justified from by the law of Moses." Acts 13:38-39

Only in Christ are we justified. Only in Christ are we forgiven. We cannot clean ourselves up before coming to Christ. We are spiritual corpses who cannot raise themselves from the dead. He wants us to come *just as we are.* In fact, in Ephesians 2:8-9 we are told: ..."it is by grace you have been saved, through faith—and this is not from yourselves, it is the gift of God—not by works, so that no one can boast." But the next sentence, verse 10, says we're created in Christ Jesus "to do good works, which God prepared in advance for us to do."

We are in Christ *to do good works.*

Some people try to choose either *faith* or *works*—but the Bible clearly teaches that faith and works go hand in hand; they're one. We've been saved by grace, through faith—to do good works! When we study to show ourselves approved, we see that genuine, living faith does not turn back or turn away. Genuine faith seeks God and moves forward toward Him, with Him, and in Him, producing clear evidence of itself: good works. Anything else is not true faith—it's called demonic, and *dead.*

> "We are not people who turn back and are lost. Instead, we have faith and are saved." Hebrews 10:39

> "So it is with faith: if it is alone and includes no actions, then it is dead. But someone will say, 'One person has faith,

another has actions.' My answer is, 'Show me how anyone can have faith without actions. I will show you my faith by my actions.' Do you believe that there is only one God? Good! The demons also believe—and tremble with fear. You fool! Do you want to be shown that faith without actions is useless? How was our ancestor Abraham put right with God? It was through his actions, when he offered his son Isaac on the altar. Can't you see? His faith and his actions worked together . . ."
James 2:17-22a

Living Faith

Living things have action, growth, production, and reproduction. On the other hand, dead things degenerate until they rot away. As they decompose, their corruption spreads, damaging whatever they touch. Some grime is dangerous—and it cannot be removed without a pressure-washing. In the same way, the poison of sin damages and corrupts what it touches. But God, in His mercy, takes us through pressure and trials to purify us. Let's read from Revelation again. Take special notice of what "fine linen, bright and clean" stands for:

"Let us rejoice and be glad and give him glory! For the wedding of the Lamb has come and his bride has made herself ready. Fine linen, bright and clean, was given her to wear. (Fine linen stands for the righteous acts of the saints.)" Revelation 19:7-8

As we saw in the last chapter, the context of God's "never leaving or forsaking us" is important. Exploring it in depth shows that He will never be the first to walk away. If we remain with Him, He'll remain with us. Explore the concept in depth and you'll also find that He's willing to take His people back and to forgive them if they repent and turn away from their unfaithfulness—in other words, wash their robes.

> "Happy are those who wash their robes clean and so have the right to eat the fruit from the tree of life and to go through the gates into the city. But outside the city are the perverts and those who practice magic, the immoral and the murderers, those who worship idols and those who are liars both in words and deeds." Revelation 22:14-15

> "Let the wicked forsake his way, and the unrighteous man his thoughts: and let him return unto the LORD, and he will have mercy upon him; and to our God, for he will abundantly pardon." Isaiah 55:7

> "But because you are lukewarm, neither hot nor cold, I am going to spit you out of my mouth! You say, 'I am rich and well off; I have all I need.' But you do not know

how miserable and pitiful you are! You are poor, naked, and blind. I advise you, then, to buy gold from me, pure gold, in order to be rich. Buy also white clothing to dress yourself and cover up your shameful nakedness. Buy also some ointment to put on your eyes, so that you may see. I rebuke and punish all whom I love. Be in earnest, then, and turn from your sins." Revelation 3:16-19

We are in Christ to do good works.

Jesus wants to clean you up and clothe you in fine linen, which stands for righteous actions. These are free clothes, provided entirely at Christ's expense. He wants to heal your blindness too—and this is all free! But He rebukes and punishes those He loves. You must repent and remain in Him:

> [Jesus said] "You have been made clean already by the teaching I have given you. Remain united to me, and I will remain united to you. A branch cannot bear fruit by itself; it can do so only if it remains in the vine. In the same way you cannot bear fruit unless you remain in me. I am the vine, and you are the branches. Those who remain in me, and I in them, will bear much fruit; for you can do nothing without me. Those who do not remain in me are thrown out like a branch and dry up . . ." John 15:3-6a

Look back at Revelation 22 on the previous page: We read that only those who have washed their robes have the right to eat from the tree of life and enter the gates. The perverts, the immoral, those who practice magic or worship idols, and liars (either in word or deed) remain outside, in death. They refused to let Him heal them and clothe them in good works. Most of us have felt the decaying power of sin in our lives, through our actions or the actions of someone else. But have we let Him heal and clothe us? Living faith regenerates and cleanses us; are you being regenerated and cleansed?

Have you washed your robe?

The Warning

In Revelation Chapter 3 Jesus warned the lukewarm that He would spit them out if they did not repent. In John 15 He warned that those who do not remain in Him will be thrown out. Scripture is filled with warnings. But people are weak, and most people begin their faith journey with an inadequate understanding of the gospel. They do not know how to live their new life in Christ. They are easy targets for their old nature, lying spirits, false prophets, and blind guides.

There's nothing wrong with being a baby, but babies who don't grow are terminally ill. While in the baby stage, you might have separation anxiety when you sin.

When the devil tricks you, or your emotions, desires, or lusts take control (and you do something you know is wrong), you might feel separated from God's Spirit. Unless your heart is hardened, you'll feel convicted or guilty about your sin. At that point you have two choices: you can admit that you're unworthy, then repent and cry out for Him to forgive and change you, or you can pretend that nothing's wrong.

If you want to pretend, you'll have the support of many false prophets, heretical teachers and blind guides.

But If I parade through town with only the clothes I was born with—and other *unclothed infants* clap—does that mean nakedness really is acceptable? Newborns do not know any better, but I hope you understand it's unacceptable. Certainly the Scriptures are clear: We will not be welcomed in to the wedding of the Lamb without our wedding clothes.

Here's what Jesus said about (and to) the most well known, respected religious leaders of his day:

> "How terrible for you, teachers of the Law and Pharisees! You hypocrites! You sail the seas and cross whole countries to win one convert; and when you succeed, you make him twice as deserving of going to hell as you yourselves are! How terrible for you, blind guides!" Matthew 23:15-16a

The Pharisees were considered the *good guys* of their day—they were the most outwardly religious men in town. They kept the Law of Moses much better than we do. But they were not united with Christ—they missed the purpose of the Law: It was meant to bring them running to Jesus. The Law of Moses was intended to show them their need for the promised Savior. The Pharisees rejected Christ and most of them died separated from God. Even their converts were destined for hell. But their religious type is not yet extinct—and they're still teachers. The apostle Paul warned us about the day we live in:

> "The time will come when people will not listen to sound doctrine, but will follow their own desires and will collect for themselves more and more teachers who will tell them what they are itching to hear. They will turn away from listening to the truth and give their attention to legends." 2 Timothy 4:3-4a

Christ's Spirit enables us to please God. The same Spirit also wants to warn us when we're being lied to—but we must be listening. False prophets and hypocritical liars become more common every day. Their lies are unnaturally clever—because demons thought them up. When these men and women mimic the Holy Spirit, they're very convincing. Unless we continually surrender to the Holy Spirit and stay in step with Him, we're no match for false spirits and deceivers.

Do you remember *Theresa*, the young woman I was briefly engaged to? There's more to that story that you should know. In about 2004, Theresa and her husband (let's call him *Demas*) returned on vacation and I saw her at church. She looked miserable. We spoke briefly and she asked me to pray for her marriage. I may have prayed, but in those years I had my back to God and my ears plugged. My prayers were ineffective. But years later, seven or eight years after my life was transformed, Cheryl and I noticed Theresa and Demas's presence on the Internet and we connected briefly. Demas's sermons were online and went back many years. I could now see that as young men, we had been similar, but not identical. As a young man Demas often reminded himself of God's promise to never forsake him. But I'm not sure Demas realized that those comforting promises had an equally strong flip side; God promises that if we turn away and walk in stubborn disobedience, He most assuredly will forsake us. This is one place where Demas and I differed: I had seen both sides of that vow when I was a young man—it was not comforting because I frequently walked in stubborn disobedience.

During Demas's many years as a pastor, he often admitted that he was a naturally sinful man who found himself "stumbling" into disobedience, anger, jealousy, lust, and pride over and over again. But his response was different. *It's not my fault*, he said. *It's Adam's fault. I was born this way. It's the Law's fault—it produces evil desires in me.* Demas admitted that each time he went near the Law, it produced another sin. Instead of concluding that he was separated from God and should not presume to be a teacher until he found a solution (we who teach will be judged more strictly), Demas came up with a new theology he called "the way of grace." His plan was to avoid the Law because it produced sin. *Separate from it or divorce yourself from it,* he taught. *Focus on the finished work of Christ.*

Now, I firmly believe in focusing on Jesus and His finished work. But Scripture declares that the Law is perfect and blameless. We have no legal grounds to divorce the Law. Therefore, without a death, we will remain married to the Law and separated from Christ—no matter how much we gaze longingly toward Jesus on the cross. Demas and I might have started out alike, but when we looked into the mirror of Scripture and saw our condition, we responded differently.

> "Does this mean that by this faith we do away with the Law? No, not at all; instead, we uphold the Law." Romans 3:31

Scripture says that by faith *we uphold the Law.*

But Demas missed that. Like many men who fill pulpits in these last days, Demas decided that the apostle Paul was not talking about "life apart from Christ" in Romans Chapter 7 when he said, *"I don't do what I would like to do, but instead I do what I hate . . . I know that good does not live in me—that is, in my human nature. For even though the desire to do good is in me, I am not able to do it."* Demas had been taught that Paul was speaking of his former condition and was thanking Jesus that he was now free from the control of his flesh. But Demas rejected that interpretation because he himself was enslaved by the desires of his flesh.

Likewise, Demas had been taught that Chapter 8 shows there is no condemnation *"for those who are in Christ Jesus, who walk not after the lusts of the flesh, but after the Spirit,"* but as he aged, he refused to believe this verse meant he needed to stay in step with the Spirit. He refused to believe he'd be condemned if he walked *according to the lusts of his flesh*. Accepting that interpretation would mean believing he was not actually living a Christian life!

Instead he rejected the things he had been taught and developed a new belief system, which he taught to his large church and sizable Internet following. Demas and I might have been similar as very young men, but by the time we matured, our beliefs were polar opposites. In fact, listening to the man preach, you might conclude he had read everything I just wrote in this book and was arguing against me—accusing me of twisting the Scriptures and teaching *lies from the devil.*

I do not share all of this for my sake, but to defend the gospel. Too many men today preach half of the gospel—but as I mentioned, a half-truth is also known as a falsehood. If I did not know the Scriptures and had not already tasted the beauty of being free to choose righteousness (through surrendering to Christ— *moment-by-moment, all day, every day, 365 days per year, which equals 31.5 million seconds per year*) maybe I would have been swayed by the man's convincing arguments. But the power of being united with Christ (31.5 million seconds per year, for many years already) had transformed me, and kept me transformed. Christ's fruit (LOVE) grew continually in my life as I yielded to Him—and I knew it wasn't because I was trying harder to be better. *I was never that good!* No clever preacher could erase this proof.

> "Some people get caught in their sins right away, even before the time of judgment. But other people's sins don't show up until later. It is the same with good deeds. Some are easily seen, but none of them can be hidden." 1 Timothy 5:24 CEV

Some time around 2014, we heard bad news about Theresa and Demas. They had left their church followed by rumors of a scandal with a pregnant mistress. They firmly denied any wrongdoing, but as more things surfaced, it became harder to give our friends the benefit of the doubt. People from their congregation said Demas and Theresa had moved his mistress into their home and called her his "second wife." She eventually ran off, they said, leaving her baby for Theresa to raise.

When I heard these things, I was grieved for their family and reminded of the potential for evil I had seen in my own nature. I thanked God that my wife had replied something like, *Over my dead body!* each time I had proposed anything sinful for our family or marriage. Now as I prayed for our friends and their devastated congregation, I knew I must always continue to deny my old man, to be dead to myself and alive to Christ—moment-by-moment—so that I could remain free to be a slave to righteousness. God knows I did enough wrong during the years I fought against His Spirit—I thanked Him for giving me a wife whose convictions had made me nervous. In His mercy, He restrained me and kept me from showing the world what I was really made of.

As we continued to pray, it became nearly impossible to believe our friends were being falsely accused. Although no longer a pastor, Demas still taught the Bible through his popular website, accepting donations to his sermon ministry—but he did not confess (or mention) there that his faulty doctrine had devastated his congregation and his family. And he kept preaching the same exact message. Also, on the side, the couple wrote songs and played live music in bars (yes, you read that correctly). Their original lyrics were cold-hearted and disturbing. One very graphic song told about an evil woman who *led men into sin*. "She's evil," they sang. "It's her fault that daddy put a bullet in his head." The song repeated the theme, *It's not my fault. It's all her fault.*

Soon reports said Demas was being accused of much more than just an inappropriate relationship: The police did not believe the mistress had really run away. She was missing, yes, but Demas was being accused of murder. He vowed his innocence over and over again, but at last he was offered a plea bargain—if he would just show them where the body was. Demas took the deal and led them to a grave on his property.

But for the grace of God, there go I. In other words, if I'm separated from the power of God's Spirit, I could end up in the same sorry condition, destroying many other lives along the way. A natural man does not have a resurrected life, because he refuses to die to himself. The natural mind cannot understand spiritual life, because it does not have the Spirit. A natural man is no match for his flesh, or the devil. And a natural man should never presume to speak for God Almighty— who will not be mocked.

> "My name is the LORD! I won't let idols or humans share my glory and praise." Isaiah 42:8 CEV

Jesus said that those who *do what God wants* are His family. Receiving the Holy Spirit is simple. God freely gives spiritual gifts—for the common good. But looking like you have a spiritual gift proves nothing. The proof is in whether or not you *do the will of God*.

As we saw in the lives of the Corinthians, some people just need to be educated. But fruit is important—and if the fruit of God's Spirit (selfless love) is not evident in a man's life, there might be much more going on than a simple lack of understanding. Remember, pirates have always flown *friendly flags* (instead of displaying their true colors) to get within close range of their potential targets. We must *test the spirits* and *examine the lives* (fruit) of those who claim to be teachers of the gospel. If Cheryl had known this when she was a young believer, she could have avoided me—thereby avoiding a lot of pain in her own life. If my friends in those old days had known to look for God's fruit, maybe they wouldn't have followed in my faulty footsteps.

Remember, God will not force His Spirit or His transformation on us. Allowing Him to tear us down and build something new—for His glory—is a continuous choice.

The supernatural life means living in a state of brokenness. Repent means to turn around and change our mind whenever our will is not aligned with Christ's—it results in a heart change and a change of actions. We do not repent only once, or even occasionally. Our corrupt nature is the opposite of God's perfect nature, so we

must surrender *moment-by-moment, 24/7, 365 days a year.*
Do you remember how many seconds that is?

Conclusion

As I end this book, I hope I've at least given you reasons
to ask God to reveal the whole gospel to you. As I
mentioned in the introduction, I've heard people use
the phrase *What Would Jesus Do?* And I've seen many
wear the *WWJD* bracelets to remind themselves to ask
this question before making a decision—and this is a
good thing. We really should care what Jesus would do
and we should do the same.

But what would Jesus do?
And how would He do it?

Jesus would be filled with the Holy Spirit, without measure. He would surrender to the will of the Father, by the Spirit's power.

Jesus is choosing a people for Himself. He's clothing
them with His righteousness. His chosen people are His
dwelling place and His body. Paul said, *"Don't you
know that your body is the temple of the Holy Spirit...?"*
Notice he doesn't say it's a lemonade stand with gospel
tracts setting out. It's the actual dwelling place of God's

Spirit. But let's be honest—put aside the self-delusion: You cannot be a dwelling worthy of God's presence without *true grace.* And I'm not talking about the so-called grace that false teachers peddle while hiding their skeletons. I mean the grace of a God who raises the dead and transforms them into the image of His glorious Son.

Do you want His power in your life? Surrender to Him today—and keep on surrendering *moment-by-moment.*

"Come as living stones, and let yourselves be used in building the spiritual temple, where you will serve as holy priests to offer spiritual and acceptable sacrifices to God through Jesus Christ. For the scripture says, 'I chose a valuable stone, which I am placing as the cornerstone in Zion; and whoever believes in him will never be disappointed.'"
1 Peter 2:5-6

"In the past you were spiritually dead because of your disobedience and sins. At that time you followed the world's evil way; you obeyed the ruler of the spiritual powers in space, the spirit who now controls the people who disobey God.

Actually all of us were like them and lived according to our natural desires, doing whatever suited the wishes of our own bodies and minds. In our natural condition we, like everyone else, were destined to suffer God's anger. But God's mercy is so abundant, and his love for us is so great, that while we were spiritually dead in our disobedience he brought us to life with Christ. It is by God's grace that you have been saved. In our union with Christ Jesus he raised us up with him to rule with him in the heavenly world." Ephesians 2:1-6

Author
Contact Information

His Power can be purchased in large discounted quantities. To order, or to contact the author for speaking engagements, write to:

Mike Ellicott
c/o Sweetwater Still Publishing
SweetwaterStill@gmail.com

www.sweetwaterstill.com

NOTES

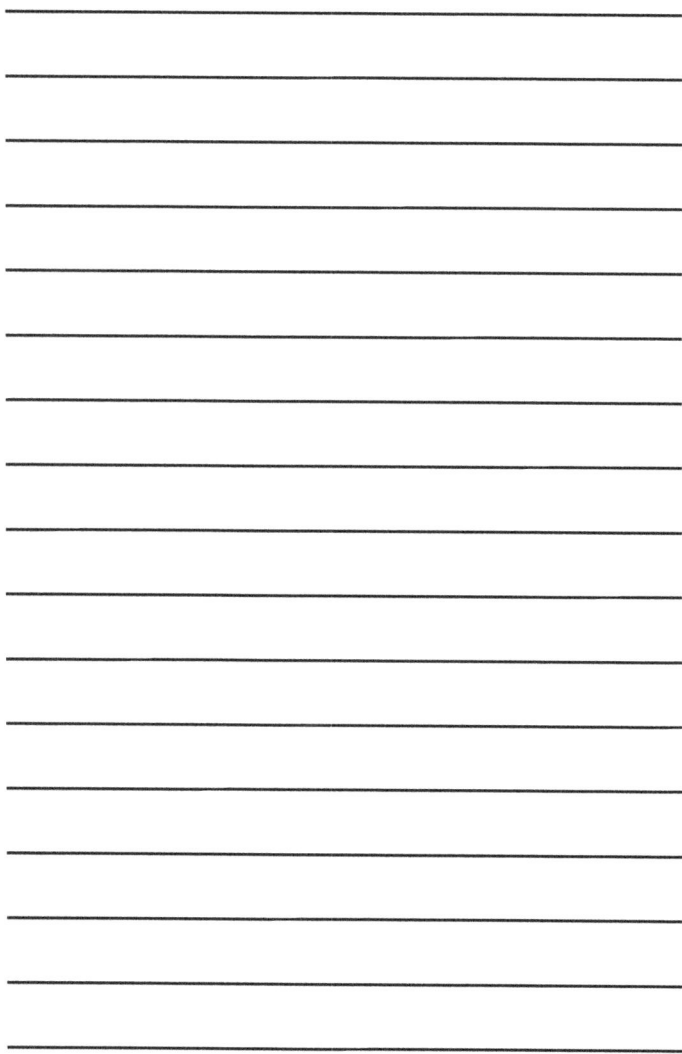